MW00535077

BIGGER THAN TINY
SMALLER THAN AVERAGE

SHERI KOONES

GIBBS SMITH
TO ENRICH AND INSPIRE HUMANKIND

For my loving family, Rob, Alex and Jesse

First Edition
26 25 24 23 22   5 4 3 2 1

Text © 2022 Sheri Koones

Front cover photo: © 2022 Gaffer Photography
Back cover photos:
    Top left © 2022 Mark Woods Photography
    Top right © 2022 Brett Hitchins
    Middle © 2022 Aaron Montoya
    Bottom left © 2022 John Cole
    Bottom center © 2022 Henry Gao, Red Dot Studio
    Bottom right © 2022 Joe Fletcher Photography
    Author photo © 2022 Annie Watson
Additional photographic credits are found on the opening page
of each chapter.

Published by
Gibbs Smith
P.O. Box 667
Layton, Utah 84041
1.800.835.4993 orders
www.gibbs-smith.com

Designed by Ryan Thomann

Printed and bound in China

Gibbs Smith books are printed on paper produced from
sustainable PEFC-certified forest/controlled wood source.
Learn more at www.pefc.org.

ISBN: 978-1-4236-5845-0
Library of Congress Control Number: 2021945201

CONTENTS

INTRODUCTION

After years of bigger is better, the trend in home building has started shifting away from extra-large houses to smaller ones. As many homeowners began working at home during the Covid-19 pandemic of 2020–21, some city dwellers opted to pack up and head for the suburbs. Now, even though most can return to the office, many people continue working from home. For some, it's because employers are giving them the option; others just don't feel comfortable returning to crowded elevators, open offices, and busy streets.

For those who left cities to avoid having to mingle with the masses, the decision was easy since they were being told to work from home. Many saw it as a temporary move. But then along came another shift, one that would permanently blur the lines between home and office. Companies learned that employees were often just as productive, some even more so, when they worked from home. They also started doing the math and realized that eliminating or downsizing the physical office could save them a lot of money. Some were pleasantly surprised to find out that when employees "lived" at the office, less time commuting translated into increased productivity and oftentimes happier, less stressed, employees. As a result, many companies have since altered their future plans, deciding whether it even makes sense to bring employees back to the office full-time, part-time, or at all.

As a result, vacation or country homes have become full-time dwellings for some families, while other homeowners are exploring their options should they decide to permanently opt out of city life. Homebuilding and real estate sales are booming as lifelong city dwellers look to build or buy houses in suburban or even rural areas of the country. Designers are taking notice and coming up with plans that include work-from-home spaces for students and workers.

The *Butterfly Garden Cottage* on John's Island, South Carolina.

BUYING SMALL FOR ECONOMIC AND SOCIAL REASONS

The trend toward smaller homes is not limited to one specific generation, and, while economic considerations are a major factor, they are not the only ones. While a large percentage of today's college graduates are entering the housing market with massive student debt, marrying later if at all, and having fewer children later than previous generations, in many cases they are deciding to live smaller due to their active lifestyles. They'd rather spend a Saturday afternoon going for a bike ride or a jog than mowing the lawn or fixing a leaky pipe. Eating out has replaced dinners at the dining room table. Travelling to new and exotic locations, and posting about it, is the perfect vacation for many.

But, in some cases, a newfound respect for the environment is driving the trend toward smaller homes. Younger generations have already grown up with energy-efficient light bulbs, recycling, and electric cars—constant reminders of their responsibility to create a smaller environmental footprint. Often these values are taken into consideration when deciding on a future home.

In the case of empty nesters and active seniors, after raising their families in homes as large as they were able to afford, many are looking for a lifestyle change. Often the move is based on a desire for a completely different location or a climate that is suitable to activities they plan to enjoy during retirement. Others want to ditch the staircase for ranch-style homes with the entire living space on one floor. Another group would much rather spend time and money traveling and staying in shape than on home maintenance.

In many parts of the world, people buy or build homes with the intention of living there for a lifetime. That mindset is finally beginning to take hold in this country. Even younger buyers with small children see themselves aging in place. They

The *Triple Barn House* in Sonoma, California, is 1,751 square feet but feels much larger with well-designed spaces for company and privacy.

recognize that if they build a large house, it will outgrow them once the kids move out, so many are choosing homes that are simply "big enough."

A DIFFERENT USE OF SPACE

Many of today's homebuyers are interested in more practical spaces that will get plenty of use. Cavernous rooms filled with "stuff" are being reconsidered for spaces that lend themselves to informal gatherings of family and friends. Homeowners no longer want space that will rarely be used except as a place to store more stuff that will rarely be used. Growing up in a small house myself, we had a living room and dining room that were only used when we had company. Today there is a different attitude about space; people want space that is usable and multifunctional. Living rooms have been turned into multimedia rooms. Dining rooms and breakfast areas are often one and the same and can also function as workspaces. Workstations are being built into hallways, and offices often double as guestrooms. Bumpouts and niches are built into floor plans for private areas and workspaces. There is more focus today on making every part of the house functional.

In this small accessory dwelling, the *Glad House*, a workspace was curtained off to add a bit of privacy.

The owners of the *Bohicket House* built an ADU where their children could be home-schooled.

As a growing number of people work from home, either full- or part-time, there is a bigger emphasis on developing workspaces into the home's design plan. This includes students who've been learning remotely and, even when back at school, will still need places at home to do their work. The *Little Black House* has two workspaces—one on the landing and a niche on the first floor. Even in the small accessory dwelling unit (ADU), the *Glad*

House, a small curtained-off work area was incorporated into the plan. The owners of the *Bohicket House* built a small ADU for home-schooling their children.

There is also a focus on enlarging common areas and making bedrooms smaller. In the *Bohicket House* they built small bedrooms so the family could focus on spending quality time together in the common areas.

SEEKING NEW ENVIRONMENTS

Whether moving from the city to the country or suburbia to a rural environment, many people are seeking a different way of life. While some are looking to get away from the chaos of a city, others are looking for the opportunity to be part of a community to avoid feeling isolated. The owner of *M's House* was seeking just such a community and found one in a home adjacent to a condo area with gathering spaces and nearby neighbors.

The homeowner liked the idea of being part of a community, although hers is a private house and the others are townhouses. The rear of her house is just beyond the Arcadia shared garden. (Photo courtesy of Rick Keating)

WAYS THAT DESIGNERS MAKE SMALL HOUSES FEEL BIGGER

There are many ways to design a smaller house so that it feels larger than it is.

Built-ins have become increasingly popular because they save space. In the *Micro Home* there is barely any furniture. Most of the furnishings, such as the couch and storage areas are all built-in.

Exposed framing in the ceiling of the first floor and a vaulted ceiling on the second floor make the *Scott House* feel larger. Outdoor space is especially important in small houses as it expands the limited indoor living area. All of the houses in this book found creative ways of constructing comfortable outdoor spaces. The *Bow Hill House* and others have several outdoor spaces for expanded space and private time.

Here are some other strategies used to make houses feel bigger:

- High ceilings
- Light colored cabinets and walls
- Open floor plans
- Well-placed windows
- Creative storage
- Open staircases
- Rolling barn doors
- Pocket doors
- Minimal hallways
- Dual-purpose furnishings
- Porches and patios

Most of the furniture in the house is built-in, including all kitchen storage.

ENERGY EFFICIENCY IS UNIVERSALLY DESIRED

Energy efficiency was a major factor in all the small homes profiled here. Passive heating and cooling were incorporated into most of the houses. Some of them were positioned on the lot for maximum solar orientation, some included high-efficiency glazing, with optimal window placement. High-efficiency insulation along with ENERGY STAR appliances and high-efficiency heating and cooling systems were also part of the structure of many of the houses. Several of the houses have solar panels—some are off the grid, such as the *Passive House LA,* or are capable of being independent of the grid, such as the *Bellingham Prefab House.*

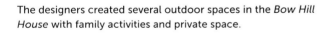

The designers created several outdoor spaces in the *Bow Hill House* with family activities and private space.

The *Passive House LA* has solar panels and a backup battery and is designed to function off the grid.

The owners of the *Hygge House* were more concerned about quality over quantity and built this 832-square foot house with the best quality materials and systems, such as high-efficiency windows and high-quality appliances.

QUALITY OVER QUANTITY

Many of the homeowners in this book said that they wanted quality over quantity in the construction of their homes. They prioritized spending money on energy efficiency and high-quality and sustainable materials rather than having space they don't need. The *Micro Home* is a great example; built with custom-made, high-quality cabinetry and other fine materials, it is only 430 square feet. The *Hygge House,* just 832 square feet, was built with high-quality materials.

The *Alley Cat* accessory dwelling unit was designed to be low maintenance with metal siding and roofing.

The *Coach House* was transformed from a run-down structure to a gorgeous residence in Washington, DC.

AN EMPHASIS ON LOW MAINTENANCE

Low maintenance materials were another priority for the homeowners featured in this book. A number of the houses have standing seam roofs, which require minimal maintenance and are long lasting. There are also several houses with steel siding or framing to stand up against the elements. The *Passive House LA,* the *Alley Cat* and the *Triple Barn House* have metal siding. The *Bohicket House* was built with prefabricated insulated metal components to endure a marine environment.

In order to find the small home of their dreams, all the homeowners in this book either had to build it or remodel one with good bones and potential. Their homes are unique, designed to live larger than they are, and built with attention to design, sustainability, and function. Most of them sit lightly on the land with reverence to the environment in which they exist. I hope they will inspire the reader to consider the potential that small efficient homes provide.

ACKNOWLEDGMENTS

This book has been particularly meaningful to me as I have lived through and watched the world change. Our priorities, methods of working, and life itself have changed during the pandemic. I started working on this book before it began but did a good deal of it while quarantining at home. The homes in this book became even more relevant as time went by and I saw the changes in people's work habits and at-home experiences.

I am so grateful for all of the time that the photographers, architects, and homeowners shared with me and for their photos and stories provided for this book. A special thank-you to my friend Peter Chapman for help beyond the call of duty. I am so appreciative of the fine work on the graphics by Chuck Lockhart. He has been through several books with me and always executes meticulous floor plans in the most delightful way. My gratitude to Madge Baird for her enthusiastic support for this book, Ryan Thomann for his beautiful book design, Merri Ann Morrell for page composition, and Leslie Stitt for her fine editing. Thank you for the support of my family—Rob, Alex and Jesse. This has been a labor of love, and I thank all of you who have made the process work so well.

COACH HOUSE

RENOVATION

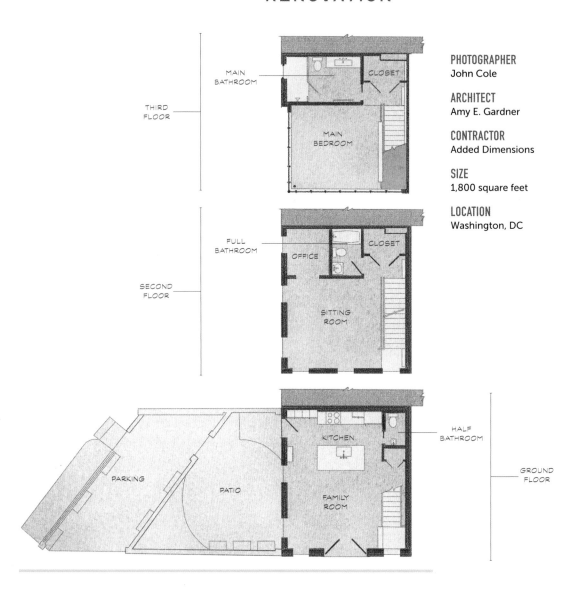

PHOTOGRAPHER
John Cole

ARCHITECT
Amy E. Gardner

CONTRACTOR
Added Dimensions

SIZE
1,800 square feet

LOCATION
Washington, DC

Opposite: The exterior of the house was designed to fit the massing and design of the other houses on the street, and the new windows retain a historical look. After removing masonry to reveal an original opening, a local craftsman custom fabricated the double carriage side door that opens to the alley.

Beth-Ann and her husband Carmen Gentile inherited this property from her mother. When these empty nesters decided their large barn-style house in Cleveland Park was too large, they decided to renovate this property, which had once been a coach house. Amy Garner was highly recommended to the couple to make their vision for the house a reality. And they needed her to design a third-floor addition to make the house a livable, downsized alternative for them.

GREEN FEATURES

- Restoration of existing structure
- Green roof
- Recycled materials
- Quartz countertops

ENERGY FEATURES

- Heat pump
- Induction cooktop
- LED Lights
- High efficiency insulation
- On-demand hot water heater
- High efficiency windows
- Low-flow faucets and showers

Above: The custom red coach doors emulate the original look of the house as well as those in the area. The open floor plan gives the home a more spacious feel than it would if divided up. The change in ceiling materials defines the kitchen from the living room area.

RENOVATION REQUIREMENTS

The couple had to have the extra floor to make the project work for them. They also needed bathroom facilities on each floor—a half bath on the first floor, full bath on the second, and main bathroom on the third floor. They didn't want to lose the history of the house—a coach house/garage in an alley—and they wanted to preserve some of the rough features such as the garage door in the living room, exposed ceilings, and exposed ductwork. They also wanted the exterior to reflect the house's modest origins.

According to Gardner, the couple sought to enhance the scale of the house on the avenue, giving it a presence where it had little to none before. They wanted a modern kitchen, rich in Chinese color, to contrast with the raw, exposed character of the space. Since the west façade of the house was windowless, they needed to bring light in along the west wall, which they accomplished with the creation of a skylit staircase zone.

A redesigned courtyard provided outdoor space and a place to park their electric car. All of this renovation, says Gardner, "needed to include a sustainable agenda including the adaptive reuse of the building, on-site stormwater management under the courtyard, an efficient building envelope, all LED lighting, and a green roof."

Left: The front door of the house opens into the kitchen on the first floor. It is glazed to admit light and is painted red to coordinate with the Chinese red just inside the kitchen. The floors of the entire first floor are porcelain and the countertops in the kitchen are quartz.

Below: The first-floor plan is open, with light coming in from several windows and the glazed front door. The ceilings have the original wood joists and beams, with new framing added where necessary to accommodate the renovated design.

A LONG HISTORY

The original coach house, constructed between 1907 and 1911, was a two-story brick structure that served as the garage adjacent the mansion built in 1905. It is situated on an alley and a major avenue, Florida Avenue, with a courtyard between the building and the avenue. The building which is approximately 25 X 22 feet is of robust load-bearing masonry and wood frame construction.

Prior to the lot being designated as part of the historic district in the 1980s, the structure was converted to residential use and subdivided to be on its own lot.

The building is set back from the property line with its courtyard enclosed by a six-foot-high brick wall; a second lower brick wall separates a parking space from the sidewalk. The coach house, in orientation and distance, is fully removed from the avenue on which it sits. It has no rear yard or windows on the rear property line, and thus is dependent on the alley and the avenue sides for its light and view.

Left: The staircase between the three floors provides a commercial element to the home. This design allows light and air to flow between the floors and gives the areas a more open appearance.

Above: The second floor has a sitting room with a small office nook (not seen in the photo) and a bathroom. The flooring on both the second and third floor is engineered, reclaimed red and white oak.

Opposite: The third-floor bedroom is light-filled with two giant window systems (one on the east wall and one on the north wall) with windows all joined together. The windows have two kinds of glass: one translucent and the other transparent. Skylights over the steps bring in additional light to this area.

RENOVATING A HISTORICAL BUILDING

Renovating such a historic building is not without challenges. Since the property is in a historic district, they had to get approval first from the local Advisory Neighborhood Commission and then from the Historic Preservation Review Board (HPRB). Before getting those approvals, Gardner sought guidance during the design process from a staff member of the DC government's Historic Preservation Office. The review process took about six months until the HPRB approved the design and then it took about fifteen months to complete the renovation.

The Gentiles say they had never undertaken a major renovation project before and had heard nightmare stories about such projects going wrong. However, Beth-Ann says, "With Amy's design and her careful monitoring of the construction as well as our excellent contractor and outstanding construction superintendent, we never had a serious problem or misunderstanding even though we were away from Washington for large chunks of time during construction."

MOVING FROM TOO BIG TO POSSIBLY TOO SMALL A SPACE

Although Beth-Ann had misgivings about making this radical move from a too large house to what looked like a too small one, over time she has made the transition. "I admit there are times I would like more space—and the pandemic has been a test. However, we have a lovely, private courtyard and a dedicated parking spot in front of the house and all the conveniences of in-town living. The rewards have outweighed the risks."

Although the house is just three rooms and 2½ baths, each room is good sized and has definite character, with the large main bathroom offering unexpected serenity. Beth-Ann says the downside to a small house is the lack of an attic or basement for storage. She quips, "Living in three rooms is like living on a sailboat." However, her old house with its unlimited space had become a storage area for family members as well as for unused stuff. It took about nine months to have massive amounts of belongings either hauled away or distributed to their daughters. She allows that there may still be another round of culling in the future.

Above: The main bathroom on the third floor is luminous and spacious. The trough sink eliminates the need for a second sink.

PARING DOWN IS A PROCESS

The process of getting rid of things forced the couple to figure out what they wanted to put in the new house. By the time they moved, they had distilled an eclectic array of furniture, artwork, and collections to enhance their three rooms. Except for buying a new bed (with storage), they furnished and decorated the house with items they already had.

Beth-Ann says, "The pandemic has made us appreciate our courtyard even more than pre-pandemic. We have lovely landscaping that has somehow matured in the two and a half years, and a large stone patio enclosed by a six-foot-tall brick wall that shields us from traffic noise. Our dog would prefer more space but it's just fine for two humans."

ELECTRIC VEHICLE SUPPLY EQUIPMENT (EVSE OR CHARGING STATIONS)

In 2019 there were about 245,000 electric vehicles sold (according to Statista.com) in the United States. The Edison Electric Institute (EEI) projects that number to reach 18.7 million (or 7 percent of EV) by 2030. The EEI also predicts about 9.6 million charging stations will be required to support this growth in EVs. Electric cars are clearly a growing trend in this country as people decide to limit their footprint on the planet by reducing the need for fossil fuel. Having an electric car requires a charging station, which is what the Gentiles installed in their courtyard. Their EVSE is hardwired back to the house and a charging cable plugs into the car. The actual battery charger is on the vehicle. Clipper Creek was the supplier of the EVSE installed.

The purpose of the EVSE is to monitor for electrical safety, maintain communication with the vehicle, and make power available at the vehicle's request. It is not the charger, but it is required to get power to the charger. Some of these stations are installed outside and some inside, while some are hardwired to the junction box in the house and others are direct plug-in. These stations work with most vehicles; however, Tesla provides their own adapter for their cars. A weather-proofing box is necessary for a plug-in version for exterior installation, and an electrician should be consulted before installing an EVSE to make sure the house has enough power for the station.

BELLINGHAM PREFAB HOUSE

PANELIZED

PHOTOGRAPHER
TJ Simon,
www.the-creativeco.com

DESIGNER/MANUFACTURER
Stillwater Dwellings
www.stillwaterdwellings.com

GENERAL CONTRACTOR
Chuckanut Builders
www.chuckanutbuilders.com

SIZE
1,634 square feet

LOCATION
Bellingham, Washington

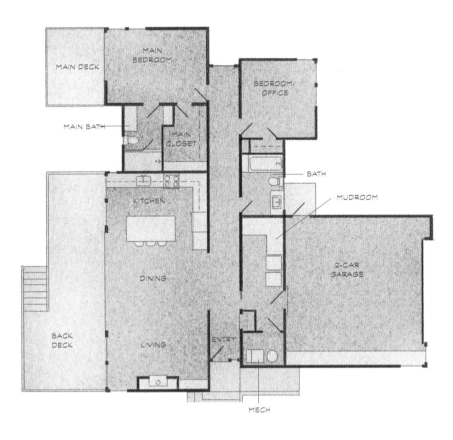

Jay and Dina wanted to downsize and build a house with a view of Bellingham Bay where they could age in place. They wanted it to be within Bellingham city limits for sewer and water utilities and have convenient access to shopping, restaurants, and other services. Their goal was to build a highly energy efficient and sustainable home on one level, with at least a half-acre of land.

Above: The house is designed with glazing throughout, providing lots of natural light and ventilation. The extended roofline blocks out the sun in the warm months and allows in the sun during the cooler months when the sun is lower in the sky.

GREEN FEATURES

- Heat recovery ventilator (HRV)
- Low VOC finishes
- Native and edible landscaping
- Metal roof with recycled material

ENERGY FEATURES

- Photovoltaic (PV) panels
- High efficiency water heater
- Large overhang
- Mini-split heat pump
- ENERGY STAR appliances

Above: The living room is a cozy sitting area with a direct vent gas fireplace for cool days. The fireplace has a remote control with a thermostat.

BUILD PREFAB

After doing on-line research into home construction options, they decided that building their house prefabricated was going to be their best choice. They found Stillwater Dwellings were constructing the modern, environmentally friendly type house they were hoping to build. After attending a Stillwater webinar and meeting with its CEO, Kaveh Khatibloo, Jay and Dina decided this was the perfect company to build their home.

Since Jay and Dina were novices at building a new house from scratch, they particularly appreciated the guidance they got from Kaveh and the Stillwater team, including finding them a terrific general contractor.

FINDING THE PERFECT LOT

Kaveh helped the couple look at potential properties that would be appropriate for their needs, eliminating those that were too expensive to build on, those with easements and setbacks that would make it difficult to build on, and those with other red flags. When they saw a three-quarter-acre property that met all their criteria, Kaveh checked it out and they jumped on it within hours of its listing.

Right: The long hallway off the common areas opens into the private areas—the bedrooms and bathrooms.

Below: The living room, dining room, and kitchen are all open concept with scenic views of the beautiful foliage and mountains.

Above: A multipurpose room functions as an office or as a second bedroom when there are guests.

Opposite, top The large deck vastly expands the living space of the house.

Opposite, bottom: The PV panels on the roof provide much of the energy required to run the house. The siding for the house is cedar and the roof is standing seam metal. A stone path leads around the house to the garage, decks, and other outdoor space.

BUILDING ENERGY EFFICIENCY

The couple knew they wanted solar power and the greenest heating, cooling, and air- and water-handling systems available. Their general contractor helped them choose a local solar company and a heating, ventilation, and air-conditioning (HVAC) subcontractor to help with those choices.

Since their photovoltaic panels produce more energy than they need in the summer, they get credit for the excess power their panels produce for use in the darker months. After the credit is used, they pay for the power over and above what the panels produce. They say their annual total energy bill for gas and electric is about $900, with electricity $800 and gas $100. They also get an annual solar production incentive from Washington State which is about $2,500 a year. This incentive payment offsets the electric bill and leaves them with a surplus of about $1,600.

Their home is highly efficient with ENERGY STAR rated appliances, high efficiency windows, a heat pump for heating and cooling, high efficiency water heating, and a heat recovery ventilator (HRV) to ensure fresh air circulates, which is important in such a tight house.

AGING IN PLACE

The house was designed on one level with easy access so it could be the couple's forever home. They have stairs and an ADA-compliant concrete ramp to their front door for any eventualities that may happen. Although they generally enter the house from the garage with a step-up, they say that area can be modified with a ramp if necessary. The kitchen was also designed with easy open and soft close drawers and cabinets and touchless faucets. Doors in the house have no knobs to turn, making them easy to maneuver.

Above: The side outdoor deck looks out on the Bellingham Bay and the Canadian islands beyond.

A PLACE FOR EVERYTHING

Jay and Dina say that when they downsized, their goal was to take only what they needed or really wanted and to avoid putting anything in storage. In order to take what they ultimately wanted, they needed to have a good deal of storage space. The cabinetry throughout the house was custom built to their specifications, so everything is just where they want it and easy to access.

The couple says the house feels much bigger than it actually is. They especially appreciate the ceiling-to-floor windows in their great room, where they spend most of their time. They were seeking beautiful views from their new home, and they say that looking out at Bellingham Bay and the Canadian islands is exactly what they were hoping for.

PANELIZED CONSTRUCTION

Panelized construction is a fast-growing prefab method used in home construction as well as commercial projects. Wall, floor, and roof components are produced in a factory, numbered for assembly, trucked to the site, and then installed like a jigsaw puzzle. Some panelized homes arrive on site with windows, doors, siding, and roofing installed and others have those components installed on-site, depending on the house and the manufacturer.

Building with panels produced in a factory is an ideal form of construction since the panels are built in a protected environment and are not dependent on local weather conditions. Prefab factories also have access to more sophisticated tools and machinery, speeding up the production time, and creating less waste, much of which can be recycled. While the framing is clearly faster and more straightforward in a factory setting, all of the subcontractors—including plumbers, electricians, and insulation installers—still have to be managed on-site when the wall assembly arrives. Ultimately there is a cost savings in time, labor, and materials. One comparison study of two identical houses built side by side (one site built, the other panelized) found several remarkable statistics. The panelized house had a 75 percent reduction in man-hours to frame, 25 percent reduction in the amount of lumber used, and 75 percent reduction in scrap generated.

BULLY HILL HOUSE

SITE BUILT

PHOTOGRAPHER
Brad Feinknopf/OTTO

ARCHITECT
Studio MM Architect, PLLC
www.maricamckeel.com

GENERAL CONTRACTOR
Terrance Fink, Teb Fink Building
www.tebfinkbuilding.com

STRUCTURAL DESIGN CONSULTANTS
Silman Engineering
www.silman.com

MILLWORK CONSULTANT
Cabinet Designers
www.cabinetdesigners.com

SIZE
1,100 square feet

LOCATION
North Branch, New York

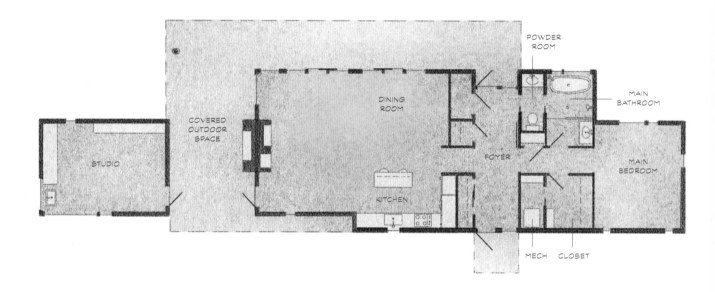

Opposite: The house is set back, hidden from the main road by a gentle hillside, in a lush agrarian setting, backing up to woods on one side with sweeping views of Bully Hill and distant mountains on the south. It is positioned with the living/dining room and main bedroom/bathroom facing south to take the best advantage of the views. The exterior of the house is a combination of 18-inch Corten steel panels and black-stained pine siding. Beautiful views can be seen from every room in the house.

After raising their children in a four-bedroom house in Long Island, Anthony and Laura Iaconetti were ready for something different. They had been thinking about retirement and downsizing for a while. They chose the Catskill region because of its natural beauty and the extensive range of activities, plus it was close to family and friends, the biggest incentive. Their focus was finding property with south-facing views for optimal solar exposure. After about two years of on-and-off searching, they came across a six-acre parcel in a beautiful, bucolic setting. It was in an open hayfield surrounded by woods on three sides and had long-range views. It was the perfect place, and they made an offer on it the next day.

GREEN FEATURES

- Corten steel siding and interior
- No air-conditioning
- Recycled shipping container for storage
- Low-flow faucets and toilet
- Recycled material
- Natural landscaping

ENERGY FEATURES

- Cross ventilation with positioning of doors and windows
- Optimal solar orientation
- Hybrid insulation system (combining both closed-cell and open-cell insulation)
- Radiant floor heat
- Large overhang
- Ceiling fans
- Concrete floors for thermal mass
- ENERGY STAR certified appliances
- Propane, high efficiency boiler

The property was part of a large working farm and the next-door dairy farmers had been using that land for many generations to grow hay to help feed their cows. When they purchased the parcel, Anthony and Laura agreed to allow the farmers to continue to farm the land downhill from their house. During the construction process the Iaconettis were careful not to disturb much of the landscape. Their excavators carefully scraped all the topsoil with hay from the area where the house would go and piled it up for use later. The shale that the property sits on was excavated to construct their gravel driveway. Once the house was complete, the soil containing the hay seeds was returned to the area. Their landscape plan was simple: maintain the original hayfield with a mowed walking path around the home.

Above: With Laura's love of cooking and Anthony's love of eating, the kitchen is the hub of the house for gathering together their large family or hosting casual gatherings of neighbors and local farmers.

NEW GOALS AND NEEDS

Their main goal was on downsizing and having a place to focus on their interests and hobbies, as they eased into retirement. Laura says, "We wanted this house to be low maintenance, with low energy requirements, and serve as a quiet retreat with a creative working environment." They say they no longer had a need for as many material things as they had previously had and wanted to shift their focus to "life experiences and self-fulfillment."

Below: A large Corten-faced fireplace with a built-in wood stove anchors the main living space, which has an open concept living area. The whole house is flooded with light by the multiple clerestory windows, massive movable and stationary windows, and multiple operable doors. The flooring is concrete, adding thermal mass and limiting the heating and cooling required in the house. Furnishings are sparse and functional.

Right: The shower/bathtub space is a growing trend originating in Japan. It offers the opportunity to relax in the tub and then clean off in the shower without leaving the immediate area.

Above: The separate art studio is a flexible creative place for Anthony and Laura to focus on their personal hobbies and interests, which include photography, painting, yarn dying, knitting, soap making, among others.

WORKING WITH AN ARCHITECT

Anthony and Laura were delighted to work with architect Marica McKeel of Studio MM and her team. The homeowners say that the firm was very client-focused in its approach and talked with them about their goals, project requirements, design preferences, and construction budget. They reviewed design development drawings together and then chose their preferences before final plans were competed. The couple were complementary in their approach to the project, with Anthony focusing on design, while Laura was all about practicality and functionality.

Every design detail was worked out prior to the start of construction, and Anthony and Laura were included in every aspect of the build from choosing the builder to staking out the house, deciding the best direction for it to face, rusting the siding, shopping for granite, and meeting with builders and contractors. It took over two years from the time they met with McKeel to the house's completion.

PRIORITIZING LIVING SMALLER AND CREATING A FOREVER HOME

Large public spaces were a priority for Anthony and Laura, and they focused on maximizing the public spaces where they would spend the most time, while minimizing private spaces. These larger common areas allowed for small gatherings of friends and family. Storage was well thought out with a place for all their things—deep adjustable cabinets in the kitchen, lots of shelving in the studio, large walk-in closets, and a good-sized pantry. They recently purchased a used shipping container for storing all their outdoor furniture, tools, and equipment. Anthony said it was liberating getting rid of the things that they didn't need or even forgot they had. Anthony and Laura appreciate the lack of clutter around this very well-designed space.

Aging-in-place was another priority in designing the house. Anthony wanted a two-story house to obtain maximum views; however, Laura's practical priorities won out. The one-story house would work better for them in the future. It had to be low maintenance, energy efficient, and cost effective to function well in their retirement. The majority of the exterior is clad in a maintenance-free Corten steel panel system to withstand the harsh Catskill winters.

Another necessity was a workplace for their creative endeavors, fine arts for Anthony and fiber arts for Laura. They like that it is separated from the living space and offers them a private space to work.

Top The house is set on a large open field surrounded by beautiful foliage and mountains.

Above: The covered patio with a firepit is a relaxing place to enjoy a glass of wine on cool days.

Above: The rear of the house has large overhangs, which prevent the house from getting too hot in the summertime. In the colder months when the sun is lower in the sky, the house benefits from the solar energy.

Their favorite thing about the house is its connection to the outdoors. "The views are amazing, with the house organized to give glimpses, rather than give it all away at once," Laura says. "Each area of the house offers different views and ways to connect to the outdoors." They love the beauty of the Corten steel and the well-designed kitchen.

This home is a true open concept plan; there aren't even doors to close off the bedroom from the public space. Although it is much smaller than their previous home, due to careful planning they say it doesn't feel small. Since there is no basement or attic for storage, they are learning to live as minimalist as possible.

Laura says, "We love the gentle summer breezes that pass through the space between the house and the art studio. The overhang of the roof on the south side of the house gives us more sunlight in the winter and less in the summer, enabling the use of low man-made energy with higher natural energy. The way the house was thought out, positioned, and built made it unnecessary for central air-conditioning. Our architectural team was diligent in thinking ahead, and planning and building accordingly."

WEATHERING STEEL
OR CORTEN STEEL

Weathering-type steel combines alloys that are meant to develop a rust exterior, which acts as a protective coating if the material is left untreated and exposed to the elements. Its protective surface layer, or patina, protects it from further corrosion and makes it more rigid. Weathering steel is often referred to by the trademark CORTEN or COR-TEN steel, which is manufactured by U.S. Steel. Weathering steel exhibits increased resistance to atmospheric corrosion compared to other types of steel and eliminates the need for painting and rust-prevention maintenance. Exposure to humid subtropical climates or water pooling on the steel may destabilize the coating, however, leading to corrosion. Weathering steel is best used in a dry environment and on a structure with adequate drainage.

Corten steel siding was used on the exterior and interior of the home with the addition of black-stained pine. The interior Corten steel was weathered prior to installation on-site by the architecture team and the clients. They used vinegar, salt, and hydrogen peroxide to pre-weather the panels so they could be installed on the fireplace in their finished state.

The exterior Corten was allowed to weather naturally after installation on the house.

OAK HILL HOUSES

ON-SITE/PREFABRICATED

PHOTOGRAPHER
Gaffer Photography (unless
otherwise noted)
www.gafferphotography.com

ARCHITECT/BUILDER
Dan Rockhill and Students
Studio 804
www.studio804.com

SIZE
965 square feet—larger house
615 square feet—smaller house

LOCATION
Lawrence, Kansas

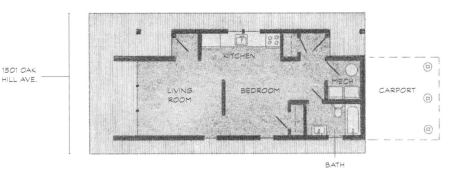

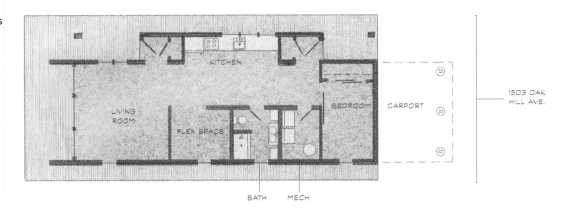

Opposite: Although one house is larger than the other, the designs are similar. Both have large overhangs to prevent overheating in the warmer months but allow the sun in during the cooler months.

This house was designed and built by Studio 804, a nonprofit organization, headed by Dan Rockhill, a distinguished professor at the University of Kansas and the head of his own architectural firm, Rockhill and Associates. Rockhill runs this unique program for graduate students at the university for "the continuing research and development of sustainable, affordable, and inventive building solutions." So far, Rockhill's students have designed and constructed fourteen Leadership in Energy and Environmental Design (LEED) structures.

Rockhill has run this nonprofit program for twenty-five years, buying land and materials and then selling the houses to finance the construction of future houses. (The program is not subsidized financially by the university.) Rockhill says, "We are the poster child for this kind of educational model, worldwide, a boot camp offered as an option to our graduate students." He usually gets about eighteen to twenty students each year, and many come to the university strictly for this experience.

GREEN FEATURES

- Fly ash used to reduce amount of cement in concrete
- Composite wood products with no added or ultra-low-emitting formaldehyde-based resins
- Ductless mini-split HVAC system
- Blown-in cellulose insulation
- Efficient wall barriers
- Infill lot
- Metal roof made of recycled material
- No-VOC interior finishes
- Residential lot rezoned as a subdivision to accommodate two houses
- Permeable driveways
- FSC (Forest Stewardship Counsel) certified wood
- Heat recovery ventilator (HRV)

ENERGY FEATURES

- ENERGY STAR rated appliances
- WaterSense faucets
- LED lights
- Triple-glazed windows

CERTIFICATIONS

- LEED Platinum
- ENERGY STAR rated
- EPA Indoor AirPlus Label

LOCATING A PROPERTY FOR THE HOUSES

For this project, Rockhill noticed a dilapidated, soon-to-be-demolished house on Oak Hill Road and discovered that he knew the demolition company that had purchased it. He bought the home from the company and in six weeks he and his students designed the two houses to occupy the space and completed the construction in seven and a half months. The houses were finished in time to host an open house on graduation weekend for the University of Kansas and for the graduating students and their parents.

Above: The houses were positioned to offer the most privacy on this small lot.

Opposite: Appliances in the kitchen are all ENERGY STAR rated. The sliding barn door creates expansive space when open but can be closed to separate the kitchen when necessary.

STUDENT BUILT

The two houses were built by the students, for the most part. With limited exceptions, they executed the design, layouts, electrical, and plumbing plans; established budgets; produced construction documents; got permits; and did most of the construction, except for some plumbing and minor work on the HVAC system. Most parts of the two houses were constructed on-site, but some components, such as the concrete formwork for the foundations, were produced in a warehouse just a short distance from the site. Off-site construction was done to avoid weather-related work delays.

Right: The expansive window in the front of the house allows in an abundance of natural light. The wrap-around patio makes the house feel much larger.

Above: The exterior design of the two houses is similar but the layout is a bit different to accommodate the smaller square footage.

ADDING DENSITY AS A GOAL

To add density to this lot, they built two houses on the parcel of land—one 965 square feet and the other 615 square feet where there had previously been one house.

The city has encouraged increased density in the older neighborhoods to lessen the sprawl of new subdivisions with the requisite infrastructure to support it. Rockhill had to create a subdivision with the town in order to split the lot and build the two houses. The two houses are similar in design, but differ in capacity and orientation, providing privacy for each on the shared corner lot. One of the priorities of this program is to address the shortage of affordable mid-income housing, which was accomplished by building the two homes, each sold independently. This high-density project is in line with the escalating population in the area and the dwindling average household size. Rockhill says, "The houses on Oak Hill Avenue reflect an effort on our part to recognize the potential of these two issues."

The other goals of this program, including these two homes, were to build for sustainability, urban infill, affordability, and assimilation to the neighboring homes.

CREATING ENERGY EFFICIENT
AND FLEXIBLE DESIGNS

As with all the Studio 804 buildings, these were built to be extremely energy efficient. The south exposure facing the street allows for a good deal of light, limiting the need for electrical lighting and cutting down on energy costs. High quality performance appliances and construction materials along with super insulation were prioritized to minimize utility costs. The simple open spaces with a restrained palette were designed to give the owner a blank canvas to create his or her own fit within it. These were the first houses built by Studio 804 that did not have photovoltaic panels. The trees on the property would have had to be eliminated for the panels to be viable. The trees, however, do provide natural shade. Both houses have vast windows for natural lighting and decks that extend the living space.

Below: Shades were installed (although were not yet in place when the photos were taken) to cut down on light and provide privacy. The purpose of the walls and roof extending five feet beyond the glass on the south side of the houses is to provide shade. Arborvitae trees were planted to add privacy.

Above: The frame for the foundation was built in a warehouse two miles from the construction site. Doing some of the components for the house in the warehouse avoided weather delays. (Photo courtesy of Studio 804)

Opposite: A space off the living room and kitchen can be used as an office or a small extra bedroom. All the furniture in the staged houses was produced by an alumni student from this design school.

THE SMALL HOUSE MARKET

Rockhill says that although small houses are not big in his area of the Midwest he has found a niche market for retirees who are interested in downsizing. The larger of the two houses was sold to a gentleman who had just retired and found this home fit his needs comfortably.

Rockhill points out that because of this program "many of his students now lead the sustainability effort in architectural firms, large and small."

FLEX SPACES

Flex spaces/rooms are particularly important in small houses where space is limited. Creating space that can have multiple uses is becoming increasingly popular and, in many cases, a necessity. The same space can be used as a guest bedroom, hobby room, exercise room, storage area, or workspace. In these days when so many people are working remotely and students are on-line learning, having private spaces for multiple family members is a necessity. These spaces can be separate rooms, part of another room, or a designated hallway space. To make the larger of the two Oak Hill houses a possibility for future owners, there is a flex room that is closed off with a large barn door.

THE LUCKI FARMHOUSE

MODULAR

PHOTOGRAPHER
Alex Farrell (unless otherwise noted)
alex@amfphotograph.com

MANUFACTURER
Method Homes
www.methodhomes.net

CONTRACTOR
Pat Bryant Construction

SIZE
1,823 square feet

LOCATION
San Juan Islands, Washington

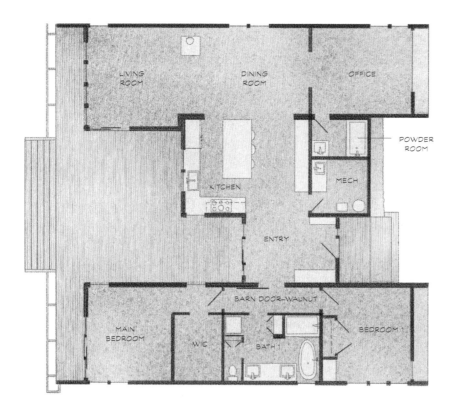

After living in Park City, Utah, for fourteen years, the owners of this house decided that their little mountain town had become too overgrown. They decided to move to the San Juan Islands, which has the small-town rural feel they wanted, only with more difficult access. They are hoping this aspect of the area will keep it from becoming too congested. With family in Vancouver, Canada, they found the Pacific Northwest has an element of "home" for them.

Above: The house was built on what was once a horse pasture with beautiful natural surroundings. To minimize maintenance and blend into these lush acres, the siding on the house is stained tight knot cedar.

GREEN FEATURES

- Low-flow plumbing fixtures
- Dual flush toilets
- Certified wood
- Drought-resistant native plants

ENERGY FEATURES

- High R-value insulation
- Heat pump hot water heater
- Heat pump for hydronic radiant heat system
- LED lights
- Solar PV system that makes house Net Zero Energy

Above: The kitchen has walnut cabinetry and oak flooring to give warmth to this modern space.

GROWING UP IN SMALL SPACES

As someone who was born and previously lived in France, the owner was used to living in smaller spaces than many people do in the United States. He said they have smaller houses there, smaller furniture, and less stuff. "I grew up with two siblings and we all five shared one bathroom. I wanted our kid to feel it was normal to share a bathroom with family, to learn to take turns . . . and to wait your turn, to learn to clean up for the next person, which are all good life lessons even if it's trying sometimes with a teen." The couple also knows that someday soon it will be just two of them, and they definitely will not need all the extra space then.

INSPIRED TO BUILD MODULAR

The family had previously constructed a stick-built house in Utah. While there, they poured through home magazines and became familiar with modular construction. When they decided to move to the San Juan Islands, they decided modular was the perfect way to build and they researched several prefab companies. When they discovered that Method Homes constructs their homes close to the San Juan Islands ferry in Anacortes and has years of experience setting houses on the islands, Method became the clear choice to build their home. Since the couple are also designers, they wanted to be involved in the design process. Their project manager, John Bacon, was happy to work closely with them in designing the custom house they were imagining.

Right: With the need for lots of storage space in a small area, the many built-in cabinets provide a place for everything.

Below: The open floor plan allows everyone in the house to be able to easily communicate. A cast-iron propane stove adds extra warmth on cool days and is particularly useful if there is a power outage. (The house is otherwise all electric since there is no natural gas piped to the island.)

DEFINITE REQUIREMENTS

The couple wanted to keep this new house under 1,800 square feet. However, they wanted this smaller house to have all the design features and efficiencies of their previous, larger Utah home. Nonnegotiable requirements were a single story, well-placed windows framing the pastoral views, and a seamless connection to outdoor spaces. The house was to be modern and comfortable.

Energy efficiency was extremely important to them. They knew they wanted a solar array on the roof, radiant floor heating, extremely efficient insulation, including an extra layer of foam in the walls, an efficient heat pump, and track lighting, rather than can lighting in the thinner angled roof areas to avoid thermal loss through the ceilings.

Above: The rear porch and nearby firepit area provide additional space for relaxing and entertaining.

Right: Photovoltaic panels on the roof provide all the energy required to run the house.

Above: The owners, having lived at a high altitude where it was difficult to grow vegetables and fruit, took the opportunity in their new house to grow a sprawling, sumptuous, albeit time-consuming garden. They grow all their own produce from spring until fall. (Photo courtesy of the owners)

Below: The modules are delivered on flatbed trucks to be set on the premade foundation. (Photo courtesy of Method Homes)

A SMALL HOUSE IS "GREAT"

The couple says they love living in a smallish house and the size of this house is great. They point out that it is cozy, efficient, easy to heat, and easy to keep clean. This family of three likes the intimacy of a small house, always knowing where they all are and having a good deal of family time together. The outside areas provide lots of extra living space in the warmer months; in colder months they enjoy their interior cozy space.

Access to outside, they say, makes the house feel bigger with big decks, a firepit area, and an orchard and garden, where they grow fruits and vegetables. Lots of windows and an open floor plan also makes the house feel more spacious. A large barn door that closes off the bedroom wing works well in separating the gathering spaces from the private spaces.

MODULAR CONSTRUCTION

Modules or boxes are built in the factory and wrapped and taken by a flatbed truck to the construction site. In most cases the modules are lifted by a crane and set on a foundation. In some cases, as with this house, the modules were rolled off the truck and onto the foundation. Some modular homes are almost complete when they arrive at the site with siding, kitchen appliances, flooring, and so on; others need a good deal of work to complete at the site.

Built indoors under strict supervision and quality control, modular homes decidedly speed up the on-site construction process, eliminating about two-thirds of the time it takes to erect a site-built home. Construction of a typical home generates around 8,000 pounds of debris, with scraps of wood, pipe, drywall, roofing, and flooring all going into dumpsters and ending up in landfills. Modular construction generates about half the waste of on-site construction, as a builder can recycle the scraps he generates into other projects or return them to the manufacturer for recycling. Manufacturers also purchase materials in bulk, reducing the energy required to make many smaller deliveries to a construction site. Because materials are kept indoors, they don't get wet or mildew. Once the modules are on site, workers assemble them quickly to protect the interior of the house from damaging weather conditions. Most exciting is that with modular construction one can build a beautiful, custom home, much like the Lucki Farmhouse.

SOLEY HOUSE

RENOVATION

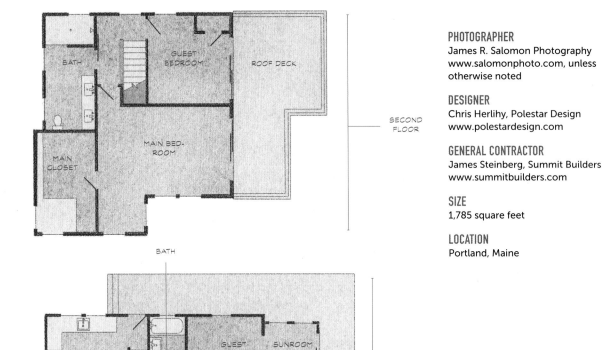

SECOND FLOOR

BATH

FIRST FLOOR

PHOTOGRAPHER
James R. Salomon Photography
www.salomonphoto.com, unless
otherwise noted

DESIGNER
Chris Herlihy, Polestar Design
www.polestardesign.com

GENERAL CONTRACTOR
James Steinberg, Summit Builders
www.summitbuilders.com

SIZE
1,785 square feet

LOCATION
Portland, Maine

Opposite: The site is covered mostly by native shoreland vegetation. The owners were able to reuse and regenerate the existing mature landscape to complement the views of Casco Bay and the mouth of the Presumpscot River. The only additions to the landscape are a rain garden to manage the water coming from the roof and a few selective shrubs for privacy. The spruce siding is painted charcoal and the contrasted portion is clear stained cedar.

Owners Olivia and Josh Soley chose this beautiful location on Casco Bay, on the southern coast of Maine, to remodel a house, not only for its views but also for its proximity to Portland and that city's amenities. Being just four minutes to Josh's office was another major advantage. He enjoys the privacy of being outside the city and the beauty and accessibility of being on usable waterfront.

GREEN FEATURES

- Reused foundation and structure
- Heat recovery ventilator (HRV)
- Locally sourced materials
- Charging station
- Low-flow water fixtures
- Natural landscaping
- Quartz countertops

ENERGY FEATURES

- High efficiency glazed windows and doors
- Electric heat pumps
- LED Lights
- Triple-pane windows

Above: Supporting the local craft community, the owners furnished the house using Maine-based companies Chilton Furniture and Huston & Company, along with a few of their own collectables.

GETTING THIS MAJOR RENOVATION BUILT

The Soley House came to fruition by saving pieces of the existing house on the property and transforming it with the help of designer Chris Herlihy, the owner of Polestar Design, and the builder, James Steinberg of Summit Builders. Herlihy, Steinberg, and the Soleys all worked together to maximize the house's potential through thoughtful consideration of how the house would be used for years to come. Herlihy says that by taking advantage of the site's natural and man-made resources, this house represents the best of its former self.

When Josh met with Herlihy, he told him that he wanted a Scandinavian-style modern home with clean lines and glass everywhere to capture the dramatic sunsets over the bay. As a commercial real estate broker and investor, he had always been interested in energy efficiency, particularly, and that had to be a priority in the building plan. He was most interested in creating a well-insulated, efficient house rather than creating energy with panels.

Left: The house has an open concept with lots of windows lighting up the whole common area of the main floor.

Below: The light and airy kitchen has multiple windows, white birch floors, white cabinets, and light quartz countertops.

DEALING WITH SHORELINE ZONING

The Soleys were able to keep the foundation of the house and some of the structure for the new house they were building. The size of the house however was limited by its proximity to the water and the existing footprint of the house that was mostly demolished.

In shoreland zoning, a house can be expanded up to 30 percent of the existing volume or the existing footprint. Designing first with 3D modeling, Herlihy was able to efficiently maximize the extra 30 percent space for the house and fit everything they needed into it.

While the house was being redesigned, shoreland regulations were changing and the city had yet to adopt the changes. Herlihy decided not to redesign the garage at that time but wait for the city to adopt the new zoning regulations that will allow for a home office or studio where the garage sat.

Left: : A daybed with storage underneath is located in the main bedroom.

Below: The bedroom and adjoining spacious deck have beautiful views of the bay.

Above: One of Josh's favorite things about the house is the second-floor deck, with the custom rail system, built to enjoy living on the water.

Right: The foundation and some of the lower walls of the original house were used to build the Soley House. (Photo courtesy of the homeowner.)

BUILDING SUSTAINABLY AND EFFICIENTLY

The original first floor wall assemblies were preserved substantially, reducing the need for using new materials. Herlihy says New Englanders are fortunate to have an abundance of natural resources for construction. Steinberg purchased lumber for framing from Dewey's Lumber and Cedar Mill, a small mill in Liberty, Maine, that sells New England–sourced products and finishes. The casework is painted New England poplar and the exterior siding is a mix of cedar and spruce from New England forests and mills.

The airtight envelope was achieved using a highly efficient water and air barrier system, triple-glazed windows imported from Germany, and high-performance doors. The Soleys' electric vehicles are charged by an on-site charging station. The LED lighting throughout the house provides efficiency and a bit of whimsy with a futuristic lighting strip that guides guests through the house to the second floor and bedrooms.

The large, energy efficient windows and the high ceilings give the home a much larger feel. The Canadian white birch flooring also lightens up the aesthetic and adds to the feeling of spaciousness.

HEAT RECOVERY VENTILATORS AND ENERGY RECOVERY VENTILATORS

When houses are built airtight, there can be a shortage of fresh air. One popular solution is a heat recovery ventilator (HRV), which can minimize energy loss and save on heating and cooling costs. The heated or cooled conditioned interior air is exchanged with the exterior fresh air, while transferring some of the heat and coolness generated in the home. Another alternative is an energy recovery ventilator (ERV), which functions in much the same way but helps to control humidity. These are more often the ventilation choices in hot, humid climate areas. For additional information, see www.eere.energy.gov.

PASSIVE HOUSE LA

SITE BUILT

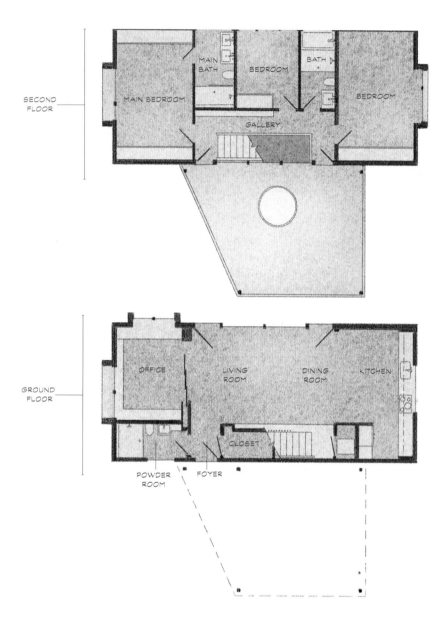

SECOND FLOOR

MAIN BATH

BEDROOM

BATH

MAIN BEDROOM

BEDROOM

GALLERY

GROUND FLOOR

OFFICE

LIVING ROOM

DINING ROOM

KITCHEN

CLOSET

POWDER ROOM

FOYER

PHOTOGRAPHER
Fraser Almeida
www.luxuryhomesphotography.com

ARCHITECT
Christopher Kienapfel
PARAVANT Architects
www.paravantarchitects.com
www.passivehousela.com

GENERAL CONTRACTOR
Guillermo Delgadillo and team

CERTIFIERS
CertiPHiers, Tad Everhart, CPHD/C
Silvia Wallis, CPHD/C

SIZE
1,750 square feet

LOCATION
Culver City, California

Opposite: The exterior of the house has standing seam metal siding (which is roofing material). A carport houses the electric car, the charging station (see page 19), and the battery that stores excess energy. The windows allow in natural lighting and solar gain in the cooler months. The most distinctive exterior feature is the fencing over the carport, which screens the sun and offers additional privacy.

Architect Christopher Kienapfel from PARAVANT Architects/ Passive House LA wanted to build a home for his family as well as create a model to highlight the strategies of International Passive House construction that he had been exposed to as an architectural student in Germany. When he began working in California, he tried several times to complete projects using the Passive House (PH) standard, but those projects did not materialize.

GREEN FEATURES

- All-electric home (no gas/fossil fuel used)
- Heat recovery ventilator (HRV)
- Infill lot development (site density increase)
- Motion sensor-activated hot water recirculation pump
- Induction cooktop
- Low-flow fixtures
- Drought-tolerant landscape and low water use plant selection
- Drip irrigation with smart sprinkler controller (weather sensor)
- VOC-absorbing drywall
- Cool roof

ENERGY FEATURES

- Photovoltaic (PV) panels
- Storage battery
- Minimized thermal bridging
- Automatic exterior venetian blinds
- LED lights
- Heat pump water heater
- Insulated slab on grade (interior floor finish)
- Heat pump condensation dryer
- Mini-split heating and cooling system (heat pump)

CERTIFICATION

- Passive House Plus*
  (*The Passive House Plus standard is a new certification by the Passive House Institute (PHI) exceeding the Passive House Classic standard. It recognizes the production of on-site renewable energy by passive buildings, requiring a minimum of 60k kWh/m2/year of renewable energy generation, plus a maximum renewable primary (PER) energy demand of 45 kWh/m2/year). 0.48 ACH @ 50 Pascals (Airtight building envelope)

BUILDING A MODEL AND FAMILY HOME

Kienapfel decided he would build one of the first certified Passive Houses in the area as a model to demonstrate the advantages of building to International Passive House standards. He purchased a small lot in Culver City and moved into the existing house on the property. He then started designing a PH to place on the rear portion of the lot. His goal was to build the most comfortable, efficient, sustainable house possible, creating a space that was just big enough for him, his wife, and child. When it was completed, he participated in International Passive House Open House Days, house tours organized by the American Institute of Architects (AIA), the US Green Building Council (USGBC) LA, as well as other trade events, showcasing his home to illustrate how a PH works and how comfortable a PH feels. The planning, engineering, and permitting phase took about one year as Kienapfel was busy attending to his architectural practice.

Above: Sixteen photovoltaic panels on the roof provide more than enough electricity to run the house and the electric vehicle. There are ten panels for the house and six for the electric vehicle.

CHALLENGES TO BUILDING A PH

He found there were several challenges to building a PH in 2013. In those days, there was limited availability to PH products and technical components in the United States. This has recently changed with many more manufacturers producing PH appropriate products, increasing competition among manufacturers, and making these products more cost competitive. In the future, Kienapfel looks forward to even more product choices available in the US mostly from the more developed European Passive House market, making it easier and even more efficient to build PH buildings. Training and education of trade professionals and governing agencies will be a critical step for the wide-range adoption across the entire building industry. According to Kienapfel, "It is only a matter of time before the Passive House will be the new normal."

Below: The lower level of the house includes the living room/dining area, kitchen, and an office that can be closed off with large sliding doors for a quiet workspace.

ESSENTIAL DAYLIGHTING

Since natural daylight was an essential component in the design of his house, Kienapfel used large windows to make the home appear much larger than it actually is. In the past PH had sometimes been associated with having limited glazing/window areas. In California everyone enjoys large windows and ample daylight, which is possible in that climate if passive or active exterior shading is used to prevent overheating during the summer months. Kienapfel figured out how to make it work by using automatic exterior blinds to pair with the large windows to control the incoming solar heat (see sidebar on page 69).

EFFICIENCY PLUS LOW MAINTENANCE

Passive House LA (PHLA+) was designed to provide maximum comfort and healthy indoor air quality while at the same time reducing the energy consumption as much as possible. This was achieved by a high performing Passive House building envelope and drastic reduction of energy consumption and then supplementing the remaining lower energy demand via a small photovoltaic system. This building is Net Zero Energy, and over the year it produces more electricity than it uses—practically becoming a Plus Energy Home. The house was also built with low-maintenance metal siding and landscaping, which is particularly important in this water-starved location.

The house has a healthy interior environment with a twenty-four-hour continuous fresh air ventilation system with air filters and heat recovery (HRV). The system supplies the living areas with fresh air and exhausts stale air from the bathroom, kitchen, and closets, with 90 percent efficiency in recovering the embedded energy without mixing airstreams or air recirculation. Since the building envelope is airtight, it is possible to control the air entering the building, filtering it (MERV-13) and removing dust, pollens, and other pollutants. If needed during the wildfire season, a carbon filter can be added to remove smoke odor from the incoming air. The patio on the second floor extends the living space of the house and provides for natural cross-ventilation between the first and second floor if desired.

Above: The bookshelves on the second floor line the gallery, which opens to the three bedrooms, one of the bathrooms, and the stairs leading to the main floor.

Opposite, top: The kitchen includes a convection oven and an induction cooktop, both which use electricity instead of gas and thus don't require unnecessary vents.

Opposite, bottom: The patio over the carport provides a comfortable and private area to enjoy the outside. The three tones of yellow add character to the exterior of the house.

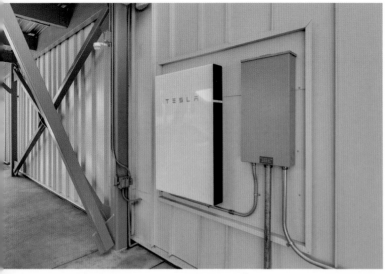

AN ADVOCATE FOR PASSIVE HOUSES

Kienapfel is a true advocate for earth-friendly living and believes PH is a positive step in creating healthier, and more comfortable and efficient buildings. PH is one of the significant contributors toward making an all-renewable, fossil-free energy grid feasible by reducing the energy demand of buildings in California. Although low energy costs have limited PH construction in the US, there has been a good deal of interest recently. The nonprofit organization Passive House California (PHCA), in Northern California, experienced an uptick when more people began working and studying from home, which sparked an increased desire to improve the comfort of their living spaces.

Kienapfel says his family enjoys the comfort of the ample natural light and stable indoor temperature all year long and the good indoor air quality. "Our child has fewer sick days after we moved into this house." They also enjoy knowing that this all-electric, fossil-free, plus-energy building has a much smaller carbon footprint and that they make a positive contribution to the environment.

Top: Just beyond the carport is the charging station for their car and the battery used to store excess energy when needed.

Above: The bathroom on the main floor has a barrier-free shower.

Right: This floor-to-ceiling wood window with aluminum exterior cladding has fixed panels and one operating tilt-and-turn window. The window spans the main bedroom and the home office. When in the lowered position, the automatic, exterior sun-protection blinds shade the large west-facing glazing.

Above: An aerial view of the house shows the original house on the property with the Passive House behind it.

BUILDING A SMALLISH HOUSE

In addition to ample space for him, his wife, and child, with sufficient space to play, there is also a guestroom for visitors and a home office. Even though there is no scenic view, the large floor-to-ceiling windows and doors make the ceilings appear taller and the interior feel bigger as the outdoors feels like an extension of the indoor living space.

Above: The exterior venetian blinds provide privacy and help block the sun during the warmer months when shade is required while also allowing in light and giving the occupants the ability to see out.

FUTURE PH PROJECTS

Kienapfel is currently working on other Passive House projects for his clients in Southern California and Australia at his architectural practice. He points out that although they are PHs, each of them is different and personalized to the occupants' needs, lifestyle, and design preferences. He sees a significant increase in interest and momentum in the International Passive House Construction Standard.

EXTERIOR VENETIAN BLINDS

Although these blinds are not yet popular in the US, Europeans have been using them for more than sixty years. These aluminum blinds help to keep the interior of the house more comfortable than is possible with interior ones. The blinds allow the house to receive natural light and see the view even when the blinds are tilted to block the sun. According to Cyril Petit of CPHBA, dealer of WAREMA, the supplier of the blinds on the Passive House LA, simulations prove that venetian blinds are three times more efficient on the outside than on the inside of the house in reducing solar gain.

The blinds can be operated manually but most are motorized and connected to a smart home automation system. They are synced to a weather station usually installed on top of the roof that has a full view of the sky and is equipped with sensors collecting all necessary information—outdoor temperature, rain, brightness of the sky, wind direction and speed, and the position of the house (GPS). The indoor temperature is also measured, using another sensor often inside the control panel, depending on the system being used. The program can automatically adjust the position of the blinds and the angle of the slats to keep the maximum natural light inside the home while preventing heat from coming in. During colder weather, the homeowner can set a comfort level with the system so the blinds will raise or orient their slats to let the sun pass through the windows and heat the room. When the comfort temperature inside the house is reached, the blinds go back down.

In freezing weather, below 32° F (0° C), ice may block the blinds and the system will send out an alert and not allow the blinds to move. The owner can cancel the alert when it is safe for the blinds to work as usual. With the slats closed during the night, an air cushion is created between the curtain and the glass that reduces energy loss. During strong winds the system will automatically raise the blinds to keep the slats from hitting the windows.

These blinds are available in fifty colors (with custom colors available) and three different finishes: satin finish, matte, or fine textured. For more information about these blinds check the website www.cphba.com

THE PINE HOUSE

ON-SITE CONSTRUCTION

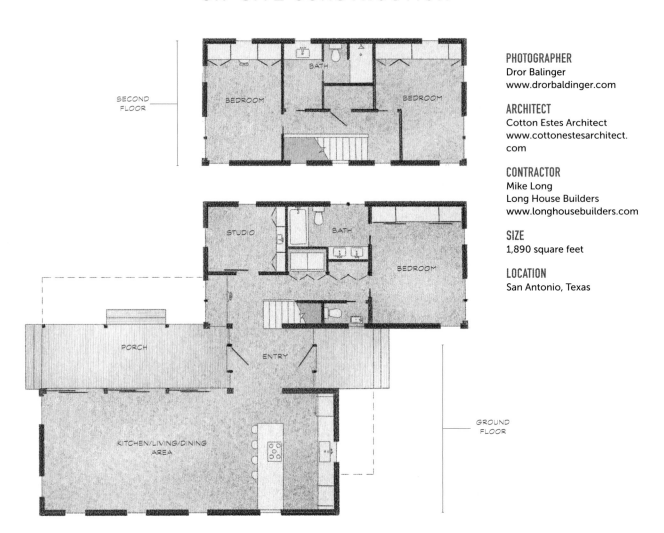

SECOND FLOOR

BATH

BEDROOM

BEDROOM

STUDIO

BATH

BEDROOM

PORCH

ENTRY

GROUND FLOOR

KITCHEN/LIVING/DINING AREA

PHOTOGRAPHER
Dror Balinger
www.drorbaldinger.com

ARCHITECT
Cotton Estes Architect
www.cottonestesarchitect.com

CONTRACTOR
Mike Long
Long House Builders
www.longhousebuilders.com

SIZE
1,890 square feet

LOCATION
San Antonio, Texas

Opposite: The siding is made from local rough-sawn pine boards. An opaque stain provides further protection for this soft wood species and highlights the rough-sawn texture of the boards. A trellised awning helps to shade the home's interior and is made from natural cedar, which is rot resistant, and contrasts beautifully with the pine.

When Sonya and Tony saw that the property next door to their own house was being auctioned off, they jumped at the opportunity to purchase it. Having lived in this downtown San Antonio historical neighborhood for fifteen years, they felt well connected to the area. However, their current home, built in 1897, was very inefficient and felt too closed in for their family of four. Sonya had spent years dreaming about a new home and what it would be like.

GREEN FEATURES

- WaterSense plumbing fixtures
- Xeriscape landscaping
- Locally sourced materials
- Rapidly renewable bamboo flooring
- Zero VOC interior finishes
- Daylight promoted with window placement

ENERGY FEATURES

- Passive ventilation
- Shade trellis awnings
- Low-E glazing
- Two-zone heat pump
- LED fixtures
- ENERGY STAR appliances
- Wired for solar panels
- Fossil fuel free

DESIGNING THE HOME WITH ARCHITECT COTTON ESTES

Just about the time Tony and Sonya were ready to build their home on this newly acquired property, architect Cotton Estes moved into the area with her partner, Mike Long, a building contractor. Sonya and Tony already had a good working relationship with Estes, having worked together on a pro-bono project for a local park improvement. Estes admired Tony and Sonya's investment in their community and felt that working with them on this new house "was a wonderful opportunity to explore how small-scale urban infill can be responsive to its setting, an important topic for a rapidly growing city like San Antonio." The project's limited budget was a welcome chance to do more with less, according to Estes.

When the couple began to communicate with Estes about designing their new house, it was clear that the young family prioritized communal gathering areas and connections to the outdoors. Because they spend most of their time between the yard, living room, dining room, and kitchen, they decided that the most space should be allocated to those areas rather than the bedrooms. The bedrooms could be small, as long as they had good light and views to the open yard. The backyard needed to have shaded areas and privacy from the street. As opposed to their previous 1897 Victorian home, their new home had to be open and bright, with free-flowing connections between the living spaces and outdoors, and with every space well utilized. They expressed an interest in downsizing their belongings and creating storage in their new home which would create a clutter-free lifestyle. They wanted their future living conditions to be conducive to family activities such as painting, cooking, and gardening.

With a limited budget, the clients wanted a home that would be appropriate for them from child-raising through retirement, when they would want limited maintenance requirements. To this end they chose low-maintenance, natural, and durable materials to weather gracefully with time. Affordable finishes and cabinetry were balanced with custom details.

Above: The entry vestibule links the front and rear courtyards. The interior wood boards are meant to mirror the exterior siding and link the interior and exterior areas of the house.

Opposite: A series of sliding doors offers a seamless transition between the interior and exterior. All openings are placed to provide ample natural light throughout the year. The double-hung windows opposite the sliding doors ensure cross-ventilation and passive cooling.

Above: A stainless steel dish-drying rack is integrated with the open shelving and drains into the sink below. This allows a view to the front entry from the kitchen, while providing easy access to daily use dishware. The butcher-block peninsula was built by a local craftsman and is made of local pecan wood.

ENERGY EFFICIENCY, SUSTAINABILITY, AND LOW MAINTENANCE: ESSENTIAL COMPONENTS

Energy efficiency was a major priority for the couple, who had lived in an old, very inefficient house. But these concerns had to be balanced with budgetary concerns. Energy efficiency was achieved primarily through affordable passive strategies, plus a performance-driven HVAC unit.

To obtain passive cooling in the summer, the house needed to be oriented perfectly. Because the family spends most of their time in the common areas and outdoors, creating a comfortable, year-round, indoor-outdoor environment was essential. The main living spaces are oriented with the long access facing south, capturing the summer breezes and winter sun. Trellises were engineered to modulate daylight throughout the year, providing full shade in summer with dappled light in the swing seasons and winter. The pecan trees provide shade to the courtyard, and offer a sense of enclosure and scale to the outdoor space.

The multi-zone mechanical system improves operational efficiency, allowing for temperatures in the bedrooms and living spaces to be controlled independently. Operable windows in every room means the family can take advantage of the colder seasons, when outdoor temperatures are favorable and mechanical conditioning is not needed. Windows in every room also provide adequate light with no electric lighting required during the daytime, reducing electrical consumption. The home is extremely well insulated and airtight, surpassing 2018 energy code (2018 IECC–International Energy Conservation Code) by 18 percent.

Estes designed the house to be as low maintenance as possible in the structural design and material selections. Natural and durable materials were chosen for their ability to weather gracefully with little maintenance. As an example, the reverse board-and-batten siding is constructed of one-inch-thick southern yellow pine with a one-inch stand-off from the house. The extra board thickness and ventilation gap help ensure that the wood siding will not rot or warp over time. Although the couple was on a tight budget, no expense was spared in the structure of the home. The foundation consists of twenty-five-foot-deep drilled piers that will resist movement over the long lifespan of the home.

Left: The built-in desk at the entry stair landing shows the consideration given to every inch of space. These custom details are coupled with affordable materials, such as pre-built cabinets and bamboo flooring. Bamboo is a rapidly renewable species that is rugged and resistant to wear and tear.

Right: The rear porch offers a comfortable environment for year-round enjoyment of the outdoors. The trellised awning, which will have plantings on it in the future, provides shade in the summer and allows slatted light to enter the interior in the cooler months when the sun is low in the sky.

LIVING SMALL

Although their new home is almost the same square footage as their old one, Tony and Sonya say it feels much larger due to the numerous connections to the outdoors, the open spaces and better utilization of square footage, and ample daylight, which is what they sought. The living-kitchen-dining room seems to expand seamlessly into the private backyard porch, patio, and yard. This creates a generous indoor-outdoor living arena with long views throughout the home, with each room offering a view of the outdoors. Thoughtful built-ins, like the desk at the entry stair landing, keep every space in the home useful and tailored to their needs. The couple wanted each area to serve multiple purposes.

Above: The rear courtyard is the anchor for family life and indoor-outdoor activities. Large sliding doors open onto a shaded porch, which steps down to a gravel courtyard, partially covered by trellis, overlooking the yard.

LIVING THROUGH A PANDEMIC

The couple joke that they would have gone crazy if they had been stuck in their old home during the pandemic. Living at this new home was a great relief to the family, and the home was extremely comfortable and relaxing for them to be in for long periods of time. They love barbecuing on their deck, and the kids collect pecans from their pecan trees. "It was really a joy getting to see our home being built from next door and having the opportunity to be at the site every day," Sonya says. In the end, she says it made it easier for them to understand the workings of the house, having watched it being built.

Estes comments, "The story of this is house is about how architecture can inspire and facilitate the daily enjoyment of life. It was wonderful to see the house come to life through their presence."

INDUCTION COOKING

First introduced at the World's Fair in Chicago in 1933, induction cooking now has about 8 percent of the market share for cooktops and ranges. An electromagnetic field below the glass-top surface transfers current directly to magnetic cookware, causing it to heat up. Induction stoves and cooktops look like regular electric ranges, but when they heat up, they do not display the glow that the other ranges do. When an induction-compatible pan is placed on the cooktop, currents are transferred to the pan and instant heat is generated. The cooktop doesn't heat up, the cookware does. As soon as the pot is removed the heating stops; the induction stovetop will not heat up unless there is a magnetic pot on it. A major advantage is the speed with which induction cooks. Induction ranges also save energy by automatically shutting off when a pot is removed from the range. This is also a safety feature, because the stove is not on when there is no pan. Induction stoves are also easy to clean. Unlike gas stoves with grills and crevices, the top of an induction cooktop is flat with minimal detail to clean. Grease and spills can easily be wiped off with a special cream, specially designed for glass-top appliances.

A minor disadvantage is the requirement to use magnetic pots. However, many kitchens are already equipped with pots that are magnetic, and these pots can also be used with any other types of stoves.

GLAD HOUSE
(GARAGE LANEHOUSE DWELLING)

ADU

PHOTOGRAPHER
Brett Hitchins
www.brettryanstudios.com

**DESIGNER/BUILDER/
INTERIOR DESIGNER**
Lanefab Design/Build
www.lanefab.com

SIZE
650 square feet

LOCATION
Vancouver, British
Columbia, Canada

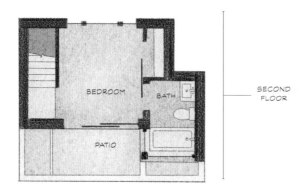

SECOND
FLOOR

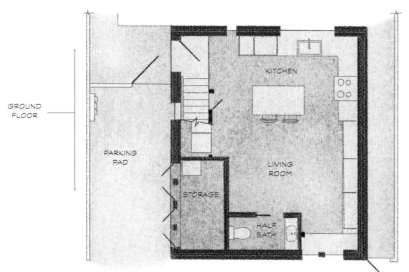

GROUND
FLOOR

Tanya and Beckie say a little patch of grass between the main house and their laneway home has given them their independence and has allowed them to maintain proximity to Tanya's parents. When Tanya and Beckie began to work with Lanefab, the designer and builder of the house, they told Bryn Davidson, the designer, that they needed their home to be a very flexible space for them to live, work, and exercise. They also needed storage for all of their outdoor gear as well as their parents' items that had been stored in the garage. Their plan was to increase the 450-square-foot garage to a 650-square-foot home when complete.

Below: The balcony on the front of the house has a large overhang offering protection from rain and strong sun. The lower white area of the house is acrylic stucco. The upper floor is clad in blue fiber cement siding to emphasize the part of the house that was added to the original garage.

GREEN FEATURES

- Reused garage space
- Heat recovery ventilator

ENERGY FEATURES

- Double wall system
- Triple-glazed windows
- Mini-split heat pump
- Tankless water heater
- Concrete floors
- Radiant floor heating

Above: The house has an open floor plan with the kitchen, living and dining room all open to each other, with a work area in a small alcove.

RENOVATING RATHER THAN DEMOLISHING

When creating an accessory dwelling unit (ADU), it is generally considered more cost effective to demolish an old garage rather than to renovate it. Because the original garage had architectural merit (designed by Marianne Amodio, an architect with MA+HG Architect), and the family wanted to preserve some of its unique features and match the main house, Davidson suggested converting the garage to a laneway house instead of demolishing it, thus maintaining the spirit of the original design. In addition, by working with the house as a renovation, the builders were allowed to forgo some of the city's design rules that would have forced the shape of the home to be less usable. To maintain some of the original design, they kept the door openings intact but infilled the space with windows and wall panels. They also kept some of the original windows.

In all, it took fourteen months to complete the construction, longer than if it had been built from scratch! A new, lower insulated slab replaced the original garage slab beneath the structure. The builders also had to install high performance windows and doors to offset the low performance of the original windows, such as those facing the yard and the large kitchen window, which were retained to keep some remnants of the initial structure. Another factor was the delay in receiving the triple-glazed windows and doors from Europe.

Below: The bedroom has a large window to bring in natural light, compensating for the small area. The large barn door alternately covers either the closet or the bathroom.

BUILDING IN ENERGY EFFICIENCY

This ADU was built to be highly energy efficient with a super-insulated double wall system that increased the wall thickness from eight inches to thirteen inches. Contributing to the efficiency are triple-glazed windows, a heat recovery ventilator (HRV) (see sidebar on page 59), and a mini-split heat pump for heating and cooling. Hot water is obtained from a gas-fired, tankless water heater.

Below, left: The home office area can be closed off with a short curtain on a hospital-style track to create a private workspace.

Below, right: When Tanya and Beckie were designing the house, they wondered about having two bathrooms in such a small space, but the half bathroom on the main floor is well used and they say it is extremely useful for themselves and their guests. The pocket door is a space-saver.

Above: The rear of the house has a porch area and an open grassy space for extending the living space of the house.

MAKING A SMALL SPACE WORK

It was a challenge to fit everything the family needed into the small space while keeping some of the original design. The height of the structure was raised, but Lanefab Design was able to maintain the boxy look of the original structure. It was a tight fit putting the storage area, entry, kitchen, living area, home office, and half-bathroom all on the main floor.

When the pandemic hit, Tanya began working remotely, spending her days at her desk at home. The south-facing window in front of the desk brings in lots of light, even on gray days, making it a very comfortable place to work. When she closes the curtain, an office space is created.

Tanya and Beckie have found the living room to be multifunctional, which is essential in a small house. They entertain overnight guests on their pull-out couch, they work out and do yoga side by side, and they host gatherings, all without anyone feeling cramped. One of their favorite parts of the home and the center of their activity is the island/table. One side of the island contains kitchen cupboards with pull-out drawers. The other side provides seating space for three. A pull-up extension leaf creates table space for an additional three people. They choose the beautiful tabletop right from the craftsman,

who they say "did an incredible job piecing it together and turning it into a work of art."

Although the bedroom is not much larger than a bed, the south-facing wall of mostly glass provides a wonderful feeling of openness. The barn door is also a space-saver.

When the house was completed, Tanya and Beckie said they achieved the creative and practical design they were seeking. They have storage in every nook and cranny they could find, including a large storage area above the stairs and a cubby at the back of their closet. Because they were able to retain the original height of the garage for at least half of the kitchen, they kept the six-by-six-foot window and added cupboards into the overhead space. They say that the high ceilings and open concept make the space feel much larger than it is.

Tanya and Beckie say they sit out on their deck almost daily in the summer. Adding a heater to the covered outdoor space allows them to enjoy this space year-round. The interior and exterior of the house worked out well for Tanya and Beckie and they are delighted with this well-planned and executed structure.

This page: The original garage was designed by MA+HG Architects. The basic shape and design of the garage were carried through to the new laneway house.

ACCESSORY DWELLING UNITS (ADUS)

An ADU is a small secondary dwelling maintained as a residence separately from the main house. It might be a house in place of a garage on the property of a family house (Detached Accessory Dwelling Units), or it can be in the basement or attached to the house as an apartment over a garage. There are several names for these types of dwellings including granny flats, in-law units, and laneway houses. In Western Canada and some other areas, laneway houses are reached from narrow alleys, which are the access roads to the garages. Legally an ADU is part of the same property as the main home and cannot be bought or sold separately; the owner of the main house owns the ADU. Often family members, elderly parents, or young adult children occupy these houses. In some places, owners are allowed to rent out these structures. There are various restrictions for ADUs depending on the location: how big they can be, who and how many can live there, and the configuration and the materials used to build them. In some areas, ADUs can help mitigate the housing shortage, increase density in the area, and help stop the displacement of individuals from previously affordable and desirable neighborhoods.

DOG HOUSE

ON-SITE CONSTRUCTION

PHOTOGRAPHER
Acorn Photographs
www.acornphotographs.ca

ARCHITECT
Solterre Design
www.solterre.com

BUILDERS
Tilia Builders
www.tiliabuilders.com
Crossridge Construction Inc.
www.crossridge.ca

SIZE
1,300 square feet

LOCATION
Nova Scotia, Canada

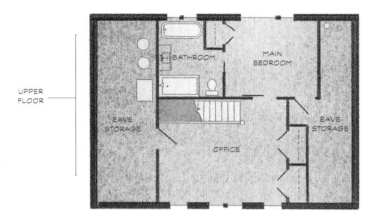

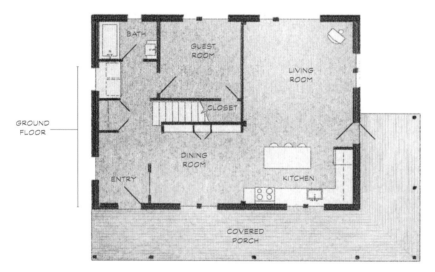

In a hamlet on the edge of the LaHave River, the Dog House sits in the midst of a small but vibrant rural community. The site has great views to the north and south and is within walking distance to a bakery, butcher, and a few artisanal stores. A nearby cable ferry connects the property to the nearby UNESCO world heritage site of

Above: The siding is locally harvested and milled black spruce board-and-batten wood. The windows and doors are triple glazed for energy efficiency.

GREEN FEATURES

- Large outdoor space
- Locally harvested materials
- Low VOC paints and sealants
- Reclaimed materials
- Metal roof with recycled material
- Heat recovery ventilator (HRV)

ENERGY FEATURES

- Optimal solar orientation
- Insulated foundation
- Concrete floors
- Triple-pane windows
- Air-source heat pump
- Super insulated

Above: With the nine-foot ceilings, the living room has an open feel with the exposed heavy timbers also adding warmth and a cabin-like ambience. The red cabinet, a focal point in the room, was built by the owner. She wanted a place to hide her television and looked for something that would be the right size. She eventually gave up and built one herself.

Lunenburg, Nova Scotia. The house is perched on a crest in a small pasture, positioned on high ground because of the challenges of shoreline construction, storm surges, and the possibility of rising sea levels. This particular location was chosen to minimize the construction's impact on the existing trees, a mix of conifers and deciduous apple and maple trees.

The owner selected Solterre Design, a Nova Scotia-based architecture firm to design the house because of their reputation in building highly energy efficient houses. Having lived in California for about thirty years, she was not used to a cold climate and what requirements would be necessary to make the house comfortable in this area. She says it was very helpful to work with a local firm who could recommend the best suppliers and who would know what works best for the location.

MOVING EAST TO NOVA SCOTIA

After visiting her brother and sister-in-law in the area for several years the owner fell in love with the region. When she learned that the property next door to them was for sale, she jumped at the opportunity to buy it and move closer to family. This property was also an ideal setting where she could have beautiful views of the LaHave River from the front of the house, and a pond and the Atlantic Ocean from the back. The house is situated on a small hill on the lot, above the main road and river, with lots of space around it for her beloved dogs to roam.

Left: The dining room looks out on the LaHave River. The owner lovingly refinished an old dining table that had been stored in her brother's barn. She says it turned out much better than anyone expected.

Below: The owner loves the open concept of the kitchen/living room and the view of the river when she's cooking or doing dishes. Simple white tile finishes are tastefully adorned with artisanal ceramics that the owner purchased on vacation in Mexico.

CHOOSING TO BUILD SMALL

The owner grew up in big houses, as did her adult children, so when she got divorced and sold her house, it was the perfect time to down-size. She bought a 675-square-foot house in California and realized that living with less stuff and less space to clean was quite satisfying. When she was planning to build this new house, she wanted it to be small as well, but big enough to host family and friends and not as spare as her most recent diminutive house in California. The smaller scale would also be more practical for her budget.

With the use of high ceilings (the main-floor ceilings are nine feet high) and many large well-placed windows, the house feels more spacious than its footprint would indicate. The large, covered porch extending the size of the house offers natural ventilation and a won-derful connection to the outdoor space. Since she works from home, the owner needed the house to feel comfortable and cozy, but also open and flexible to accommodate large family events with adapt-able spaces for extra sleeping and gathering.

The owner had three distinct requirements: a two-story house so she could take advantage of the north and south views, a rustic look, and modern, efficient construction. Building materials were kept simple, durable, and, whenever possible, locally sourced.

Above: A wraparound porch is a classic welcome entrance and provides the perfect location for a relaxing afternoon to watch the local ferry putter across the river. It was built with post and beam construction, giving it a very rustic look.

Opposite, left: The interior of the house contains many art pieces the owner collects, including this figurine she found on the beach. The thermal mass created by the concrete floors assists in keeping the house cool in the warmer months and warm in the colder months.

Opposite, right: A reclaimed cast-iron claw-foot tub, in the second-floor en suite, has a beautiful view out to the orchard.

BUILDING AN ENERGY EFFICIENT HOME

Because energy efficiency was a priority for her, utilizing passive energy wherever possible was built into the design. Solar orientation was optimized on the grassy pasture with the deciduous trees to the west, which helps prevent overheating with seasonal shading. Large, triple-pane windows in the living room not only provide natural light and ventilation but open the house up to beautiful views.

Low energy consumption and low maintenance are extremely important to the owner, not only because it makes financial sense over time, but also because of her concern for the environment. She says that while quarantining at the house for two months, by utilizing the woodstove and the sunshine, the house was warm during the day and the energy consumption was incredibly low.

Although the woodstove is small, it gives off as much heat as is ever required in the house.

The heat pump effectively keeps the house warm when heat is needed and cool in the summer during a hot spell. The thick insulation and airtightness of the house function well to keep the house warm much of the time.

According to project manager, Jordan Willett, "Efficiency, comfort, and affordability drove the envelope design at the Dog House." Balloon framing, an older form of construction (see sidebar on page 93), simplified the structure. Along with multiple types of insulation from the roof to the foundation, this technique allows for an air barrier and continuous insulation, limiting air infiltration and creating a comfortable draft-free space. On a blower door test the house achieved an excellent airtightness rating of 1.0 ACH 50 pascals (see sidebar on page 187).

Above: The house is named the Dog House since the owner has been a dog lover all of her life and welcomes the dogs of all of her friends and family to the house, including those of her builders.

Right, top: The owner built this Puppy Shed herself as a retreat while the Dog House was under construction. It is about 100 feet down a path in a clearing in the forest. It serves now as a little forest cabana for herself or the occasional guest.

Right, bottom: The interior of the Puppy Shed is rustic with no electricity or running water.

Opposite: The rear of the house as well as the grounds around the house were left natural with wildflowers and other foliage. The owner at first didn't want to cut down any of them. After moving in, she decided to plant some new foliage to ensure that the property would feel more like a nature preserve than a cleared homestead.

THE PUPPY CABIN

While her house was being built, the owner stayed with her family next door and was able to watch the progress daily. She was thankful for the opportunity to see what they were doing and get to know the house as it was being built. She had a naive notion that she could build, in about a month, a small 12 × 12-foot cabin at the back of her property where she would live the rest of the summer while the house was being completed. She didn't realize how much work it would take to build even this tiny space. It ended up taking three years to complete. Today she enjoys it as a summer guesthouse and retreat space.

BALLOON FRAMING

Balloon framing is an older style of wood frame construction where the floor is hung or attached to the side of a taller stud, which typically goes all the way to the roof. Since the beginning of the twentieth century, most houses are built using platform framing, where each floor sits on top of the stud walls, allowing the builder to use shorter timbers, which typically speeds up construction. For this house, using this old technique simplified construction and made it extremely sturdy.

HYGGE HOUSE
SITE BUILT

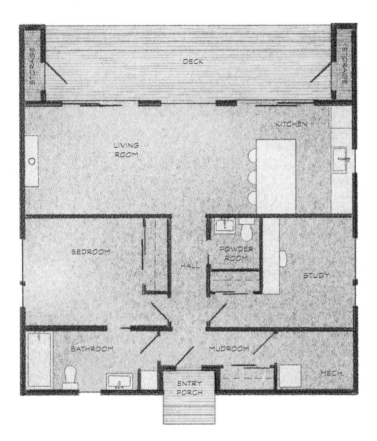

PHOTOGRAPHER
Erica Allen Studio
www.ericaallenstudio.com

ARCHITECT
Birdseye
www.birdseyevt.com

BUILDER
O'Neill Builders
www.gogreenoneill.com

STRUCTURAL ENGINEER
Engineering Ventures
www.engineeringventures.com

CIVIL ENGINEER
McCain Consulting
www.mccainconsulting.com

SIZE
832 square feet

LOCATION
Colchester, Vermont

Opposite: This lakeside house is divided into common areas with the lakeside to the west and bedrooms and utility facing street-side to the east. An extended gable with storage wing walls provides privacy, protection, and shelter for the living areas and covered deck.

Debra and Peter Maisel noticed the lack of vegetarian eateries when visiting their children who attended college in Burlington, Vermont, and knew this would be a good place for them to open a restaurant. The Revolution Kitchen would be their third such venture.

The couple were delighted to find this property located along the eastern sandy shoreline of Lake Champlain in a densely populated lakeside neighborhood. The former residence had been demolished due to water damage and the presence of lead, mold, and asbestos. This lot has a beautiful setting and was ideal because it is just a bicycle ride away from their restaurant.

GREEN FEATURES

- Low VOC paints and stains
- Low-flow plumbing fixtures
- Locally sourced materials
- Metal roof with recycled material
- Large outdoor space
- Quartz countertops

ENERGY FEATURES

- Solar ready
- High efficiency insulation
- High efficiency windows and doors
- LED Lighting
- Air-source heat pumps
- Designed for cross ventilation

Above: The kitchen, with quartz countertops, opens up to the living room.

BUILDING A PERFECT FORM FOR THE LOCATION

The couple's goals in the design were to create a well-built, affordable home that fit well into the aesthetic of the location and that maximized the available space. Their goals are reflected in the simple shape of the house with the elongated gable roof and the minimalist palette of the cedar siding and black metal roof.

Strict development regulations dictated that the new house's footprint conform to the existing dimensions of the former structure and meet the resiliency standards of the state and federal codes for structures located in a flood zone (see sidebar on page 101).

Above: The ambiance of the living area is enhanced by the gas fireplace, which keeps the entire house warm when needed.

Left: The bedroom is on the side of the house where views are less important.

QUALITY OVER SIZE

The couple was more concerned about the quality of the house than the size. They made sure that all of the materials and systems used in the house were top quality and that measures were taken to create a very energy efficient and sustainable structure. Because the house was built with airtight construction and highly efficient windows, they barely need to use their heat pump. When needed, the contemporary fireplace keeps the whole house warm. With the open doors in the living room, they get natural breezes in the summer, keeping the house comfortable in the warmer months.

Although the house is just 832 square feet, it has a more expansive feeling with the extensive glazing and the addition of the deck which is just steps from the lake. Debra and Peter say they keep the sliding glass doors open whenever possible and feel like they are outside most of the time.

Above: The two sliding glass doors add daylighting, natural ventilation, and beautiful views of the lake just beyond. The owners say they feel like they are outside most of the time when the doors are open.

Right: The house is designed to create an intimate relationship between the occupants and the landscape, which is what embodies the meaning of the term hygge. The minimalist palette of cedar siding and black metal roof feel natural and fit into the environment.

A HYGGE EXPERIENCE

Debra and Peter say the house is extremely comfortable and they delight in the views and the ambience of the area with beautiful sunsets and kites often flying over the lake. The couple named the house Hygge, a Danish word expressing coziness, charm, and pleasant feelings of well-being and positive experiences, which they say their home offers in design and atmosphere.

Above: A view to the lake can be seen at the rear entrance to the house. Parking is to the side of the entrance.

Left: The deck off the living area extends the living space while providing gorgeous views of Lake Champlain. There are storage areas on both sides of the deck.

BUILDING IN A FLOOD ZONE

Town regulations require that all projects located in a designated flood zone be constructed according to FEMA guidelines. The new home was built three feet higher than the previous structure on the property. No water can be displaced in the event of an extreme weather event, which requires the use of flood gates in the foundation walls and pressure relief valves in the concrete slab. When the water comes up to the house, the flood gates open and allow water to go into the crawl space. The slab valves admit water from below to alleviate hydrostatic pressure and prevent uplift on the concrete slab. A permanent sump pit and pump were not allowed by FEMA guidelines, so after high-water levels recede, the owners must use a portable ejector pump to remove excess bulk water. Any residual moisture in the crawl space is passively ventilated with the flood gates and the space is dried using supplemental heat conditioning.

To protect the structure from mold and mildew, all wood framing (joists, beams, and columns) within and adjacent to the crawl space use pressure-treated lumber and are protected with a mold and mildew-inhibiting paint. The floor is fully insulated with closed-cell, spray foam insulation, providing for the thermal, air, and moisture barriers between the living space and the crawl space.

An elevation certificate was required to obtain insurance, ensuring compliance with FEMA guidelines per town regulations. Architect Brian J. Mac of Birdseye, a fellow of the American Institute of Architecture concluded, "The responsibility of building a home located in a flood zone required that the design be resilient to a changing environment and climate, that the construction be durable, readily serviceable, and that the clients feel safe, comfortable, and self-sufficient in the use of their home."

MICRO HOME

SITE BUILT

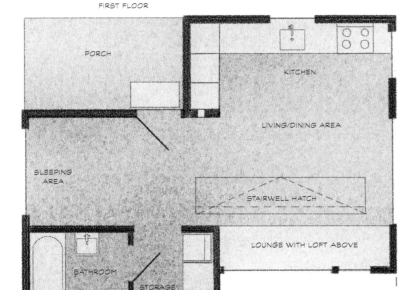

FIRST FLOOR

PORCH

KITCHEN

LIVING/DINING AREA

SLEEPING AREA

STAIRWELL HATCH

LOUNGE WITH LOFT ABOVE

BATHROOM

STORAGE

PHOTOGRAPHER
Jim Westphalen
(unless otherwise noted)
www.jimwestphalen.com

ARCHITECT
Elizabeth Herrmann
www.eharchitect.com

GENERAL CONTRACTOR
Northern Timbers Construction
www.northerntimbers.com

SIZE
430 square feet

LOCATION
Huntington, Vermont

Opposite: A light gray-stained cedar wraps the house and the roofing is standing seam metal, both requiring minimal maintenance. The yellow door adds a pop of color to an otherwise neutral palette.

The owner of the Micro Home was much more concerned with quality than quantity when he began the process of having a house built. Being a minimalist, he didn't want too much space to store more stuff than he needed. But he wanted the items that went into the house to be top quality, efficient, and low maintenance.

Although it was to be quite small, the house had to contain those important spaces that provide privacy and delineate areas. A corner was subtracted from the house footprint to form a welcoming front porch, which also helps shape the sleeping area on the inside, and the roof slopes so that the more private and intimate spaces, the bath and sleeping area, are contained under the lower part of the slope. It is also designed so that the bathroom does not open directly onto the living spaces but is approached through the built-in storage area.

GREEN FEATURES
- Metal roof with recycled material
- Daylighting
- Local resources and artisans
- Low VOC paint

ENERGY FEATURES
- High efficiency furnace
- Cross ventilation
- No air-conditioning
- Heat recovery ventilator

Above: The white concrete kitchen countertop and white custom cabinets keep the color palette simple.

Opposite: A sleeping loft is above the sitting area with the sofa/daybed, both providing extra places to sleep guests.

SELECTING A LOCATION AND ARCHITECT

Before he knew the area well, the owner house-sat in Huntington, Vermont, and quickly came to appreciate the beauty of the land, the lack of development, and its proximity to Burlington's culture and activity. After looking around the area and adjacent towns he decided that a view, easy access, and good neighbors were key. When this location came on the market it satisfied all those requirements and he purchased the land.

After seeking recommendations and then interviewing various architects, he ultimately chose Elizabeth Herrmann, partly because of her portfolio but mostly because she took time to consider all options before responding to his questions. He told Herrmann his priorities were "size, cost, and view," and then said to just "work your magic."

DESIGN DECISIONS

The materials were kept simple and light. Local maple flooring was cut in short lengths and laid perpendicular to the view giving the floor a water-like texture that makes it feel expansive and tranquil. The color palette was kept very neutral with only small pops of Mondrian-type primary colors, with a yellow door, red drum light, and blue couch/daybed.

The house was designed to have limited furniture to make the space more expansive.

Herrmann designed the built-in couch/daybed and the cabinets, and the only free-standing furniture is a single free-standing bed and table with four chairs that he already owned. The house has a designated place for everything in order to maximize space and keep the interior uncluttered.

ENERGY EFFICIENCY AND LOW MAINTENANCE

Energy efficiency and low maintenance were extremely important to the owner. He says he is not a homebody and has no desire to "tinker" with a house, so he asked Herrmann to design the house accordingly. In addition to energy efficient insulation, windows, and appliances, he wanted everything to be easily accessible and simple. He uses electric energy to heat the house but is currently considering adding solar power.

Above: The single bed is one of the few freestanding furnishings in the house. (Photo by the owner.)

Right: A hatch door is camouflaged to blend in with the floor and opens easily for basement access. The full basement stores mechanical equipment and laundry machines. (Photo by owner.)

BUILDING SMALL

The decision to build a small house was based on the owner's life-style of not owning many possessions, which, he says, can weigh you down. He would rather travel than acquire things. With a smaller house, he felt there would be less to take care of and, if he had more space, he says he wouldn't know what to do with it.

The house has a basement, which a local builder advised the owner to build. This was a worthwhile, inexpensive space to construct. It stays dry due to the excellent drainage in the area, and it provides a perfect storage area for all the utilities and the washer and dryer. He jokes that his house "is a studio apartment, with a roof and a storage unit in the country."

Below: The well-placed windows on all sides of the house provide natural light and ventilation.

Above: The house sits on an open field surrounded by beautiful foliage. The shape of the house is reminiscent of the local barns with a shed metal roof.

Opposite: Over the small table/ workspace is a red drum pendant, one of the few accent colors used for the house. The built-in sofa/daybed and wall storage units are birch plywood. The main view from the house is Camel's Hump, a Green Mountain peak, framed by a large, picture window.

FOR HIM PLUS COMPANY

The homeowner knew the house might be too small for a cumulative two weeks each year, when he has guests. Herrmann designed a built-in couch/daybed long enough to sleep two people end to end. However, because of the clever floor plan, everyone has some privacy when sleeping. He has few guests during the cold weather, and, during the warm months when his daughter and her friends visit, he pitches a six-person tent for them outside, which they love.

He says the Thoreau quote, "for my greatest gift has been to want but little," describes his lifestyle to a tee.

MAKING A VERY SMALL HOUSE FEEL SPACIOUS

It is particularly challenging to make a small house feel spacious and provide for all of one's needs. The design of this house used a variety of techniques to meet that challenge. The walls are painted white and the general palette throughout is very neutral, giving the house a very open look. Storage and most furniture are built-in, minimizing the need for furniture that would take up more space. The many windows in the house provide lots of light, making the house feel more expansive than its petite footprint.

Areas of the house are creatively separated to craft sleeping areas, creating some privacy for guests. Although it is difficult to meet all necessary needs in a small house, this one uses its space in an ideal way to make the house feel comfortable and much larger than it is.

GEORGIA CEDAR HOUSE

KIT HOME

PHOTOGRAPHER
Visually Sold, Inc.

DESIGNER
Aris Georges of OM
Studio Design

BUILDERS
Justin and Manson Peppers

FABRICATOR
Lindal Cedar Homes

SIZE
1,828 square feet

LOCATION
Chattahoochee Hills, Georgia

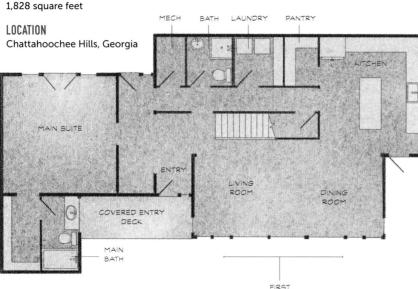

SECOND FLOOR

STUDIO/ LOFT

MECH   BATH   LAUNDRY   PANTRY

KITCHEN

MAIN SUITE

ENTRY

LIVING ROOM

DINING ROOM

COVERED ENTRY DECK

MAIN BATH

FIRST FLOOR

Anne spent several years researching the housing market in Atlanta, where she hoped to build a home. She explored teardowns in central Atlanta as well as prefab construction but didn't find exactly what she was looking for. After visiting Serenbe, an agrihood (see sidebar on page 117), for several years, she finally decided to purchase land there and build her dream house. She was drawn to the community with the farm-to-table restaurants, the countryside, and the beautiful homes and natural environment.

Above: The house is situated on a small lot but was designed with several outdoor spaces. The siding is pre-stained cedar to provide fewer emissions from on-site painting and staining.

GREEN FEATURES

- Metal roof using recycled material
- Noninvasive landscape plants
- On-site storm water control
- Passive radon vent system
- No-formaldehyde wood flooring (eucalyptus renewable resource flooring)
- Low or no-VOC interior paints
- WaterSense toilets, showerheads, lavatory faucets and accessories
- Quartz countertops
- Reverse osmosis water filtration

ENERGY FEATURES

- Geothermal HVAC
- Blower door test
- Energy recovery ventilator (ERV)
- High efficiency windows
- ENERGY STAR appliances

CERTIFICATION

- EarthCraft certified

Anne says she built this house for herself without thought of its resale value. After years of collecting ideas, she had a strong sense of her priorities and knew exactly what she wanted and needed for her home. Already knowledgeable about prefabrication, she decided to have her house fabricated by Lindal Cedar Homes, which designs and ships custom kit home packages (see sidebar on page 117). She says that her architect, Aris Georges, and builders Justin and Manson Peppers, along with the engineers and fabricators at Lindal, all helped create what she considers "a work of art," which she gets "the honor of being able to live in every day." Anne took her time in the planning stage to make sure she got exactly what she wanted. Homeowners are often burdened with many change orders during construction. She avoided this by taking the time to have all the professionals review the plans and make sure there would be no surprises.

Above: The open floor plan, large windows, and varied ceiling heights give the house an open, airy look. The wood beams and flooring add warmth to this contemporary design.

Top: The kitchen is large for the size of the house since Anne likes to cook and wanted that space to be generous. The kitchen cabinets are walnut and the countertops quartz.

Bottom: The multiple windows, including clerestory windows, along with the high ceilings, make this house feel much larger than it is.

BUILDING SMALL

Anne knew she wanted the house to be on the small side, with a modern aesthetic connected to nature. While doing her research, she was inspired by houses with varied ceiling heights defining the spaces and with the private spaces separate from the common areas. She wanted all the spaces to be functional and multipurpose, without having dedicated rooms that would seldom be used.

Anne says living in a house that is too big is a burden "in every way possible." Her first priority in building this new house was that it was smaller, with less maintenance and just right for one or two people to live in. She has felt tremendous relief and a sense of freedom in paring down and living smaller.

She says the house feels much larger than it is with the tall ceilings, vast windows, and the varied ceiling heights she was seeking. Having the

main bedroom in a separate area for relaxing and an upstairs loft for work creates a more expansive feel. The muted colors also add to the feeling of space and flow throughout the house with basically white and natural wood tones. The areas are more defined with furniture and art.

Opposite, top: Anne said she wanted her upstairs loft area to feel like she was in a tree house and, she concludes, "it does."

Opposite, bottom: The main bedroom has multiple clerestory windows that add light to the room without taking up needed wall space.

Right, top: The plants in front of the sitting area in the front of the house offer a measure of privacy.

Right, bottom: The firepit and seating area at the side of the house extend the living space and add another gathering place.

CONNECTING WITH THE OUTSIDE

Having extensive glazing was extremely important because Anne wanted the house to connect with the outdoor greenery and nature as much as possible. The huge wall of windows in the main living space is the center of the home, where Anne can see the changing landscape "like a giant moving mural." There are also several outdoor spaces that expand the feel of the house.

Above: The porch off the kitchen provides an additional dining area in the warmer months.

A DESIRE FOR HIGH EFFICIENCY

Anne wanted the house to be highly energy efficient. Because Serenbe requires geothermal systems, it helped to meet her desire. This form of heating and cooling is quiet, with no air-conditioning units and heat pumps working in the neighboring houses. Passive solar methods help to keep Anne's energy bills to a minimum. The large overhangs limit the heat gain in the warmer months.

With all the houses in Serenbe certified by the energy program EarthCraft, she was assured that rigorous tests on indoor air quality, fresh air intake, and heat loss/gain were run before she moved in. Since the orientation of the lot and house are well suited for solar, Anne plans to add solar panels in the future and hopes to someday purchase an electric car that will also be powered by the panels.

The owner says she loved the whole process of building her house from start to finish. She lives in this house with her current cat count of three.

AGRIHOOD COMMUNITIES

"Agrihoods," short for agricultural and neighborhood, are popping up across the United States. They are all centered around working farms and are focused on farm-to-table food and healthy outdoor living. The communities vary in size, location, amenities, and the involvement of the residents in the farming process. Typically, the houses in the communities are built to high efficiency standards and encourage a community of friendliness with town gathering places and activities that provide opportunities for interaction among the residents. They appeal to those people seeking a healthy way of life and those that enjoy living close to where their food is produced. The communities are built around a farm, growing vegetables and fruits, the way many communities have been built around golf courses. There are currently about ninety-five agrihoods in the United States, but this number seems to be growing as people become more concerned about healthy eating and having a closer connection to nature. Some of these communities, in addition to providing produce to residents, also offer some of the harvest outside the community or supply local restaurants.

KIT HOMES

A kit home consists of precut materials, either chosen directly from a catalog or customized for the homeowner's build site and lifestyle. The home kit package, containing tens of thousands of parts, is delivered to the build site and assembled there. It includes the exterior materials for the home, but not the interior finishes, plumbing, or electricity. The components are numbered, shipped to the site, and then erected by a contractor. This type of prefab construction allows for maximum design flexibility, efficiency, and cost predictability from the very start of the design process. Another advantage is that it can be shipped to far-off locations. Lindal Cedar Homes ships their components to all parts of the United States and Canada as well as to countries in Asia and Europe.

ALLEY CAT

ADU

PHOTOGRAPHER
Mark Woods Photography
www.mwoodsphoto.com

ARCHITECT
SHED Architecture & Design
www.shedbuilt.com

STRUCTURAL ENGINEER
Todd Perbix, www.twperbix.com

CONTRACTOR
Owner

SIZE
800 square feet

LOCATION
Seattle, Washington

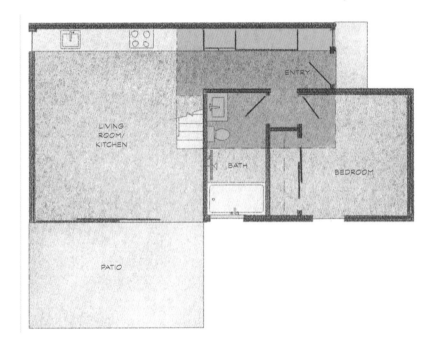

Leesa and Ben were spending a lot of time visiting family in the Southwest, and they decided their Craftsman house in Washington was more than they would need in the future. Since their area was zoned for ADUs (see sidebar on page 85), they decided to build one next to their existing home as an investment and as part of their retirement plan.

Their strategy was to build this small space, where they could live when they were in Seattle, generate rental income off their bigger house year-round, and rent out their ADU when they were out of town. However, Leesa and Ben have not moved into that next stage of their life yet. They love their ADU so much that they are currently living there and using their main home as a guesthouse for now.

Above: The siding on the house is all metal for easy upkeep and sustainability. The large aluminum slider door opens to the owners' well-kept garden.

GREEN FEATURES

- Metal siding with recycled material
- Dual flush toilet
- Low-flow faucets and showerhead
- Salvaged furnishings

ENERGY FEATURES

- Ceiling fans
- LED Lights
- Concrete floors
- Solar ready
- Hydronic heating

Above: The living room and kitchen area are wood paneled to add warmth to the interior of the house in contrast to the more industrial exterior. Concrete floors add continuity throughout the house. Both the high ceiling and its white color help make the house feel larger.

A CONTRASTING AND INTERESTING DESIGN

The couple were looking for a unique style for their ADU that was easily accessed from the alley and would have a strong relationship to their existing garden. In addition, they wanted a sun-filled interior space and main rooms on one level for aging in place. They chose Seattle-based SHED Architecture & Design to come up with a plan that was functional, attractive, and efficient.

SHED designed the house with fewer windows than usual but with highly efficient ones. Four parallel skylights in the lofted space provide daylight from above, while allowing for nighttime stargazing. There is a small window along the kitchen counter on the main floor and a well-situated bathroom window that allows in light but provides privacy. A wide, sliding glass door opens the living space to the garden and patio, preserving privacy from the main home while capturing afternoon light and expanding the living space.

It took four months to design the unit, three months to go through permit review, and twelve months to build. The couple chose to be their own general contractors for this ADU. Leesa was a skilled project manager who had building/trade contacts and was able to leverage them for her own project.

LOW MAINTENANCE AS A PRIORITY

Since the couple knew they could be away for months at a time, they wanted the house to require as limited maintenance as possible. They choose metal siding for the house because of its low upkeep and high durability. Metal was the perfect solution for the exterior since they also wanted a unique and industrial look to the structure. In contrast, the interior creates a warmer, friendlier environment.

Right: Wood paneling is carried through the bedroom area to give the house design continuity. The ceiling fan limits the need for air-conditioning in the warm weather.

Below: The well-lit loft is accessed by a custom designed staircase.

LIVING BIGGER THAN THE SMALL STRUCTURE

Despite the structure's small footprint, the living room and kitchen feel spacious due to the plentiful natural illumination and high ceilings, a design feature carried through in both the bedroom and bathroom. The interior white walls reflect light throughout the spaces creating a roomy feel while the plywood-cladding lining the rooms creates warmth and durability. Heated concrete floors establish a uniform ground plane throughout the house, while also providing thermal mass. In addition, the double-height ceilings, open layout, and natural light make the space feel larger than its 800 square feet.

Above: The large doors expand this small interior space with a seamless transition from the inside to the exterior.

Left: The wood at the entrance to the ADU creates a transition from the cool metal of the exterior to the warmer, woodsy interior. The asymmetrical roof creates space for the loft, which is flooded with natural light from the south-facing skylights. The other portion of the roof will be dedicated to solar panels in the future, which will generate enough energy to power both the ADU and the main house.

WET ROOMS

It is becoming increasingly popular to have a bathtub and shower fully open or with just a glass partisan enclosing the bathtub and shower. Bath/shower combinations have been popular in Japan for many years, where bathing for relaxation is an important part of their culture. People can take a relaxing bath and then thoroughly wash off in the shower without having to move into a chilly space.

Wet rooms have no enclosure for the shower and, in lieu of a shower tray, there is a drain where the water is directed by a gradient floor. There are several advantages in using this design. Wet room configurations take up less room when there is limited space in the bathroom and make it feel more spacious. They are also particularly helpful for people with limited mobility. These are consistent with Universal Design concepts, which require the building environment to be designed "to meet the needs of all people who wish to use it." They can also be helpful for washing pets.

A disadvantage is that wet rooms can be more costly because they require the walls and floors to be tiled and water-proofed, and the room must have adequate ventilation to avoid the buildup of humidity. They may also limit the materials used for the vanity, which is likely to get wet, and storage must be well thought out to avoid towels and toilet paper from getting soaked.

Right: The wet-room bathroom has a shower open to the tub, sink, and toilet. The well-placed small window brings light into this small bathroom while maintaining privacy.

BOHICKET HOME

PREFABRICATED STEEL FRAME AND PANELS

PHOTOGRAPHER
Tripp Smith
www.trippsmithphotography.com, unless
otherwise noted

ARCHITECT
Woollen Studio Architecture + Design
www.woollenstudio.com

MANUFACTURER
EcoSteel, www.ecosteel.com

SIZE
1,800 square feet
(680 square foot ADU)

LOCATION
Johns Island, South Carolina

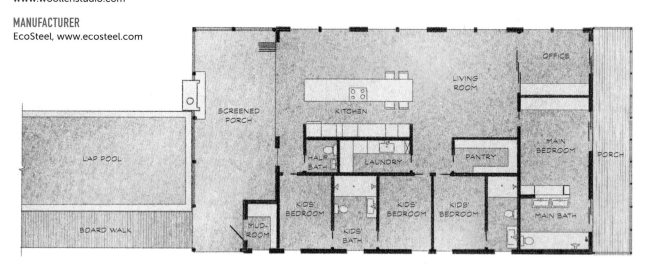

Opposite: The lap pool was added when the house was completed. It is between the main house and the ADU. The dock can be seen going to the river where the family goes to fish. (Photo courtesy of the owner.)

After seven years of living in a one bedroom, two-bath, 800-square-foot beach villa on Seabrook Island, this family of five needed more space. They bought an eight-and-a-half-acre riverfront property on the Bohicket River on Johns Island with beautiful water views. They had many ideas of how their new house should be built. Having lived in a very small space previously, they were well aware of the size of rooms they needed, and how they could avoid wasted space.

In this very traditional neighborhood, they opted to build a very modern and minimal house. In this area where many residents build large homes, they choose to build a far smaller one. They also decided to build the house with nontraditional building materials that would be perfect for this property close to the water. The house was designed with large windows encompassing seventy percent of the walls so the family could have outside views from everywhere in the house. Ninety percent of the furniture is built-in to save space.

GREEN FEATURES

- Recycled steel
- Recyclable steel construction
- Hurricane and FEMA flood-rated windows

ENERGY FEATURES

- Photovoltaic panels
- Concrete floors

CERTIFICATION

- FEMA flood and hurricane rated

Above: The kitchen, dining, and living areas are all open concept. Windows surrounding all of the rooms offer views of the exterior along with natural ventilation and daylighting.

CREATING AN INDOOR/OUTDOOR

The goal of the couple was to maximize the views to the outside. They studied where the sun was at different times of the day and seasons before deciding where the house should be placed and oriented. Positioning the driveway and walkways were also paramount in creating great outdoor spaces and beautiful water views. The driveway allows one to see the marsh and the river beyond the house, so the house gives the illusion of floating on the river. The parking area is distanced from the home allowing the couple to leave their busy life after arriving. They start their peaceful journey to their home on an elevated Ipe wood deck walkway alongside their lap pool.

Left: The living space is bright with beautiful views of the pond beyond. The couches are the only furniture in the house that are not built-in.

Below: The house extends to the covered outdoor space with a glass wall that fully opens. This area expands the living space of the house. A woodstove in the outdoor space provides warmth on cooler days.

Above: A barrier-free shower in the wet room bathroom provides a safe and convenient shower experience. It eliminates the risk of tripping while getting into a shower, adhering to the concept of Universal Design, which specifies that bathrooms should be accessible to all people at every stage of their lives.

Right: The four bedrooms were kept small to focus the space on the public areas. The beds and dressers are all built-in to save on space and help make the house feel larger.

BUILDING WITH STEEL

There were many reasons why the couple decided to build with steel construction.

Since sustainability and energy efficiency were extremely important to them, building with steel was a perfect option in this natural location. EcoSteel components were chosen for this construction because they are well insulated, create an excellent barrier from termites and the elements, and also eliminate the issue of mildew that could be a problem in this marine environment. All of the steel framing is galvanized to protect it from corrosion. Insulated roof and wall panels have an additional protective marine coating primer under the finish color.

The wife designed the house with EcoSteel and then the architects at Woollen Studio Architecture + Design came in to complete construction drawings for permitting.

Building with steel made it particularly easy to create the indoor/outdoor experience that was so important to the family. Because steel houses require fewer load-bearing walls than wood construction, larger areas of glazing are possible. The abundance of glazing provides a feeling of connection to the exterior even when the family is inside. Because the house is so well insulated with the steel panels, it is protected from overheating. Some of the windows have curtains that can be closed when necessary.

The modern appearance of the steel was also a feature they found very appealing.

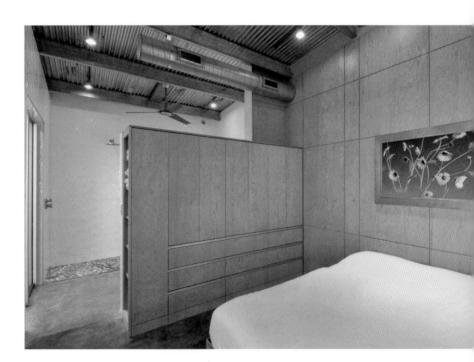

DESIGNED TO MAXIMIZE THE SPACE

The common areas as well as the children's and the adults' private spaces were carefully measured to maximize the living and outdoor spaces. Wasted spaces like halls and traditional framework were eliminated to minimize the square footage. The family enjoys the outdoors and they wanted their home to reflect their way of life. An accessory dwelling unit (ADU) (see sidebar on page 85) was built close to the house and is used for homeschooling their children and also as a guesthouse.

Bohicket Home was designed so there was no wasted space. Beds and dressers are all built-in and the only unattached furniture in the house are the living room couches. The three full bathrooms are open wet rooms (see sidebar on page 123) with wall-to-wall tile and no cabinetry. The kitchen has built-in workstations that can easily be closed behind doors. The pantry, laundry room, and main bedroom contain floor-to-ceiling cabinetry and library ladders in order to use the entire wall space. Most of the cabinets are white high gloss which reflect the outside image. The concrete floors flow continuously through the house without interruption from room to room.

Top: The family has a 24-bed garden where they grow all of the vegetables they need all year long, including tomatoes, sweet potatoes, beans, okra, watermelon, and so on. They adhere to a biointensive method of organic gardening where they grow the vegetables closer together and several together in harmony with each other so they protect each other and provide them ten times more food than an average garden, using one-tenth the water. (Photo courtesy of the owner.)

Above: Photovoltaic panels on the roof provide much of the energy required to run the all-electric house. The couple is in the process of adding additional panels to provide all of the energy needed. A backup propane generator with an auto-transfer switch is available for emergencies.

BUILDING A HURRICANE AND EARTHQUAKE RESISTANT HOME

The steel construction was a perfect solution for providing a durable, safe home that is flood and hurricane resistant. By building with steel, which can support strong wind loads, they were able to have large, impact-rated glass windows to provide magnificent views of the Kiawah River. These strong windows are transparent barriers protecting them from the elements no matter what weather conditions occur.

The house is built on concrete pilings to keep it above water in this marsh area and lift it up to provide excellent views. The twelve-foot ceilings and exposed steel beams support the wind loads and add to the interesting modern look of the house. The family of five moved in just days before Hurricane Florence hit their area in September 2018. They chose to shelter in place, and their modern steel home came through unscathed.

The house was built to be as independent as possible with a backup generator for emergencies and a shallow well system. The water is purified and oxygenated, supplying all the water needs for the house. Photovoltaic panels on the EcoSteel standing seam roof panels provide most of their electrical needs. The family is also able to provide for much of their food supply with their vast garden, eggs from a multitude of free-range chickens, fish from the river, and an apple orchard on their property.

The owners say the best things about their home are the simplicity, the multitude of windows, and its open and welcoming features. After the couple completed the house, they added a lap pool, with a black pearl pebble finish to reflect the sky and match the nearby river water.

Above: The main house is close to the ADU, which is used as a schoolhouse for the couple's three children and a guest house. Both structures are on concrete pilings to keep them above rising water.

PREFABRICATED STEEL STRUCTURES

Steel is used for home construction instead of wood because it is stronger, it can span larger spaces without requiring load-bearing walls in between, and it doesn't shrink, warp, or twist. A large percentage of steel can be recycled, and the parts can be recycled again when the structure is at the end of its life, making it a greener material. Additional advantages to using steel are its resistance to mold, rot, termites, and fire. Because steel doesn't have to be treated for insects, it also creates a healthier indoor space. When building with steel, construction time, waste, and labor costs are all reduced, and steel requires minimal maintenance. EcoSteel, the manufacturer of the Bohicket House, says the house was built with a custom-engineered structural steel frame and wrapped with an insulated roof and high-performance insulated wall panels. The prefabricated components arrived at the site ready for assembly and then all parts and pieces were bolted together like an erector set. EcoSteel's systems meet or exceed local building codes while resisting earthquakes, hurricanes, floods, and wildfires. Their systems have been used in California, which has been devastated by wildfires, and in coastal regions such as South Carolina's coastal barrier islands, where the Bohicket house is located. Their systems are engineered to secure the interior's climate regardless of exterior weather conditions.

Above: The frame was installed atop the pilings prior to the insulation and metal panels. (Photo courtesy of EcoSteel.)

SEA RANCH HOUSE

SITE BUILT

PHOTOGRAPHER
Joe Fletcher Photography
www.joefletcher.com

ARCHITECT
Malcolm Davis, www.mdarch.net

PROJECT MANAGER
Dinesh Perera
Malcolm Davis Architecture

DESIGNER
Elsa Brown
Malcolm Davis Architecture

GENERAL CONTRACTOR
David Hilmer
Empire Contracting

LANDSCAPE ARCHITECT
Floriferous Landscaping, Inc.

SIZE
1,860 square feet

LOCATION
Sea Ranch, California

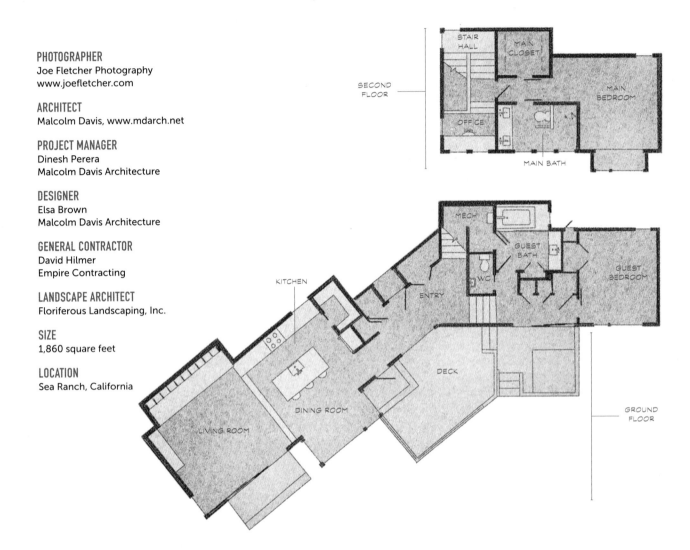

In coastal Sea Ranch, California, the owners of this house were seeking a recharging place for their busy professional lives where they could reconnect with each other and their inner selves "in beauty, comfort, serenity, and peace." They originally intended to use this home as a weekend retreat while using their Silicon Valley home as their permanent residence, eventually using this as their retirement home. However, Covid-19 drastically changed their work situations and they moved full-time to their home at Sea Ranch, where they both work remotely.

Above: The house was sited to take advantage of the stunning ocean views. The multiple levels follow the site's steep topography.

GREEN FEATURES

- Fire-resistant siding
- Bioremediation of gray water
- Recyclable metal siding
- Low-flow faucets

ENERGY FEATURES

- Strategically positioned windows
- Concrete floor slabs
- Operable skylights
- LED lights

Working with architect Malcolm Davis they requested a contemporary Californian home in a timeless architectural style, with materials and structural parts of the construction exposed. All parts of the house were to be flexible and functional while being resistant to wear-and-tear over time. They say the essential aspects of the house needed to be "openness, spaciousness, fluidity, light, warmth, and color." Their preference was for natural materials and color tones and they wanted to maximize the view, merging the inside of the house with the outside.

Above: The siding of the house is corrugated Corten steel and vertical cedar, which are natural and durable, both on the wish list of the owners.

Opposite, left: Creatively placed skylights provide lighting in the kitchen without taking up wall space. They also help release warm air and circulate the cool, fresh air that comes in through the lower window openings. The couple likes this window arrangement along high wall sections, which creates interesting patterns through shadows and colors over the course of the day, in addition to capturing a lot of light.

Opposite, right: A living room next to the kitchen has custom vertical grain fir cabinets and provides a comfortable space to relax.

METICULOUS DESIGN AND BEAUTIFUL VIEWS

Davis designed the house to capture the magnificent views of the rugged California coast beyond. The two wings of the house are angled at the entry, creating a shape that embraces the view and takes maximum advantage of the location on a hill overlooking the ocean. One wing houses the social living areas, and the other the private bedroom spaces. The two wings are connected by a light-filled corrugated weathering steel entryway, and the floor levels are split to gently follow the site's steep topography.

The house is designed in keeping with the regional style reminiscent of the barn-like structures found in this California locale, but with a modern twist composed of seamless material, color transitions, and minimalist detailing. The home's interior material palette consists primarily of simple elements such as concrete flooring, plywood walls, and industrial lighting fixtures. These create an understated industrial coastal aesthetic that harmoniously blends with the home's surroundings.

AN ENVIRONMENTALLY FRIENDLY COMMUNITY

The couple chose to build in this community because of its environmentally friendly aspects along with its beautiful views. The house is located in the coastal planned community of Sea Ranch in Sonoma County. The basic premise of Sea Ranch, according to the community, is to "live lightly on the land." The 2,200 houses in the community are built using materials and colors that blend in with the existent coastal zones and respect environmental ideals with natural materials and forms. The community has been carefully planned as to the location of houses, the preservation of open space, and the planned public paths throughout the community. Sea Ranch continually develops environmentally conscious interventions including bioremediation of gray water to maintain its own water supply and developing a vast community garden where produce is traded for labor.

Above, top: A small nook upstairs adjacent to the stairs provides a work area along with lovely ocean scenes. The other workspace for this busy couple is in the downstairs bedroom.

Above, bottom: A small sitting area at the rear of the house provides for a quiet place to view the ocean.

Right: The large windows throughout the house provide daylighting and magnificent views of the Pacific Ocean.

A FOCUS ON EFFICIENCY AND SUSTAINABILITY

Each element of both the exterior and the interior of the house was chosen based on efficiency as well as durability. The western red cedar on the exterior is extremely durable and naturally resistant to rot, decay, and insect attacks, thus requiring less maintenance and making it long lasting and sustainable.

The owners were focused on building a house with excellent quality and fine detailing rather than one that was too large. Their intent was to utilize as many passive heating and cooling strategies as possible. The windows were strategically positioned to capture solar gain and the concrete floor slabs provide thermal mass (see sidebar on page 139) to limit the need for heating and cooling. The operable skylights release heat and help circulate the cool, fresh air coming in through the lower windows and doors.

In addition, smart, space-saving design decisions were made to make the space feel more expansive, including providing a study space above the staircase.

Left: This window seat in the main bedroom upstairs is one of several areas in the house for reading and enjoying the view.

Right: The main bedroom looks out on the beautiful shoreline. Flooring in the bedroom is red oak hardwood, adding warmth to the large space.

BUILDING TO MEET STRICT CALIFORNIA CODES

The home construction followed the strict Title 24 California Building Standards Code, which requires "energy conservation, green design, construction and maintenance, fire and life safety, and accessibility" that apply to the "structural, mechanical, electrical, and plumbing systems" in a building.

The homeowners are delighted that Davis was successfully able to execute their vision of building a beautiful, contemporary home that has a warm, casual design while also embracing more traditional Sea Ranch elements. They say, "The house integrates very well into the landscape and, more often than not, we have the doors wide open so the inside becomes the outside and vice versa."

Above, top: The windows in the Corten steel area of the house provide multiple outlooks straight through the house.

Above, bottom:]A small powder room on the first floor with a mini sink and industrial fixtures is available for guests.

THERMAL MASS

Thermal mass is generally solid matter (although it can also be liquid) that can absorb and store warmth and coolness. Concrete, brick, and stone are examples of high-density materials that have the ability to store and release energy back into a space. In a home, flooring, fireplaces, and walls with a high thermal mass can help to heat and cool the interior space. In winter, the solar energy is stored during the day and released at night when the air temperature drops in the house. This heat released into the house reduces the energy required for heating the interior space. During the summer, heat is absorbed by the solid surfaces, keeping the space more comfortable during the day and reducing the need for air-conditioning.

Above: The concrete flooring in the house adds thermal mass, assisting in heating and cooling. The direct-vent gas stove provides heat when necessary. The large sliding doors provide light, natural ventilation, and a beautiful panorama.

TRIPLE BARN HOUSE

SITE BUILT

PHOTOGRAPHER
Bruce Damonte
www.brucedamonte.com

ARCHITECT
Mork-Ulnes Architects
www.morkulnes.com

GENERAL CONTRACTOR
Nima Pirzadeh, Nima Construction Co.
www.nimacc.com

SIZE
1,751 square feet

LOCATION
Sonoma, California

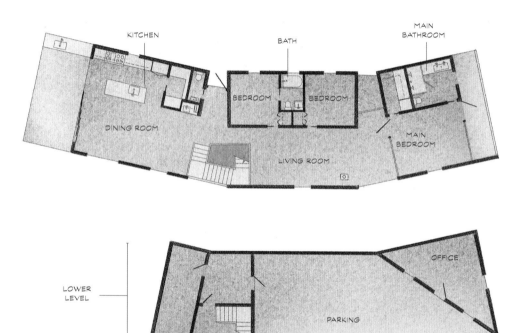

J im and Hollie Rottman were looking for a retreat and full-time residence away from a big city, where they had spent many years. The couple moved from New York to San Francisco for Jim's job as the global head of diversity and inclusion for an international biotech company. Hollie, a chef and food educator, was also excited for a new adventure and the opportunity to delve into California cuisine, specifically the growing and sustainability side of it.

Above: The house sits on the hillside with the lower concrete level containing the carport and office and the upper Corten steel levels where the living areas are located.

GREEN FEATURES
- Recyclable Corten steel siding and roofing
- Locally sourced materials
- Low-flow fixtures
- Dual flush toilets
- Electric car charging station

ENERGY FEATURES
- Optimal solar orientation
- LED lights
- Tankless water heater
- Low-E glass
- Smart thermostats
- Zoned heating and cooling

Above: One of the key features of this custom-made kitchen is the hidden pantry that stores dry goods, appliances, and the many pottery dishes, platters, and glassware the couple have collected over the years. The open-faced drawers are easily accessible for cooking equipment and daily use, keeping the kitchen space clean and spacious. A handmade walnut farm table was custom designed for the couple.

CHOOSING SONOMA VALLEY

The couple wanted a place in Northern California where they could raise their young daughter, Sophie. It would also serve as a cooking laboratory, and a relaxing getaway where they could grow their own vegetables, experiment with different recipes, enjoy Sonoma wines, and gather their friends and family.

They chose a property on a hillside, encircled by the countryside with beautiful views of the Sonoma Valley. When Hollie and Jim moved to their new home, she volunteered at the Ferry Plaza Farmers Market with CUESA (Center for Urban Education about Sustainable Agriculture) and participated in several programs to educate children about good eating and the environment. She also started the West Coast operation of the nonprofit Wellness in the Schools. Jim joined the Board of Ceres Project that provided medically tailored meals to those in need. Hollie yearned to live where she and her husband could grow their own produce, entertain outdoors, and be close to nature. The Sonoma site was the perfect place to be at one with nature but yet, within forty-five minutes, be in San Francisco, enjoying the city's art, culture, diversity, and especially the international foods they craved.

Left: The open concept allows the eye to easily see from one end of the home to the other.

Below: There are multiple seating areas in the house for a bit of solitude. The orange chair provides a sitting area between the main living area and the main bedroom. The gas fireplace is used on cooler days.

WORKING WITH MORK-ULNES ARCHITECTS

Hollie and Jim chose Mork-Ulnes Architects to design their new home, not only for their design aesthetic, but also for their intentional use of materials that create a light footprint on the land. Architect Casper Mork Ulnes not only paid great attention to the detailed design and maintaining their budget but also showed immense respect for the preservation of the land.

The orientation of the house was carefully planned to maximize the sun's positioning so the couple could rely on the wind and breezes to cool the house in the hotter months. The materials chosen were all natural and sustainable with concrete on the lower level and Corten steel on the upper levels, which blend in with the iron-red rusty soil indigenous to the area. These were perfect material solutions since they require minimal maintenance and develop more character as they age.

This Mediterranean-designed house sits on the hillside, in the shade of the trees, with gorgeous views of the tree cover, vineyards, and the mountains. The house follows the lines of the mountain, nestling easily in the terrain.

Above, top: From the lower entry level, an angular staircase leads through a concrete volume into the main residence where entrants are greeted with a beautiful view of the valley from a large picture window.

Above, bottom: Glazing is plentiful throughout the house bringing in natural light and ventilation. This is the main living space looking toward the kitchen and outside areas.

Right: The main bathroom has a spa-like appearance with a minimalist appearance: white walls, blue/gray Azul Bateig limestone tile, natural wood cabinets, and a rimless shower with multiple shower heads.

A TRIPLE BARN DESIGN

The house was designed with three roof lines defining its zones. One zone houses the public area of the kitchen and dining area as well as the outdoor kitchen and lounge. The second zone contains the guest rooms and living room, and the third zone incorporates the main bedroom and bath. With the surprise miracle arrival of Sophie, after they had designed and built the house, the couple transformed the room closest to their main bedroom into a nursery. The lower concrete level includes the entry room and stair, laundry and storage room, the carport and mandatory fire truck turnaround, and a triangular office.

The heart of the house is open with the family room and kitchen blending the outdoors with the indoor spaces. The ceiling arcs upward in a peak giving it a very spacious and open feel. The couple say they like people to be able to hang out comfortably with them in the kitchen as they cook, so there is comfortable seating in the kitchen as well as the adjoining den and outside patio. Their ten-foot walnut table anchors the space.

Although the house has a very open floor plan, it was designed with several small private nooks. These areas are not walled off but were created by purposeful design.

The materials used inside the house have a serene, natural tone. Since all of the spaces lead into each other, there is a commonality to them. The white walls keep the space bright and are enhanced by the warmth of the Douglas fir flooring and cabinetry. The colorful furnishings add a casual nature to the design.

Above: The kitchen is expanded outdoors under a large cantilevered eave which creates a shaded relief from the hot Sonoma sun. The overhang creates a continuation space for the kitchen, as the kitchen extends into the landscape with an outdoor bar and grilling area and outdoor living room.

EXPERIENCING THE WONDERS OF NATURE

According to the couple, the best thing about their home is the views. They say that every day they see something different: the fog rolls in, clouds sweep over the mountains, a hot air balloon pops up over the vineyards to the southeast of them. Hollie says, "There are hundreds of shades of green all around. The red rocks pop with vibrant reminders of the red soil clay of Sonoma. It's a magical place. Our home is a gentle guest on this land."

Top: The garden has five grow boxes, where the owners grow organic and heirloom vegetables. They try to include produce two-year old Sophie can pick and eat right from the beds. In winter they grow rainbow chard, tat soy, cabbage, purple cauliflower, broccoli, chives, rosemary, and chervil and in spring, they plant an entire bed of strawberries for Sophie. The gorgeous little alpine strawberries (*fraises de bois*) in both red and yellow are her favorites, as well as sugar snap peas. In summer, cherry tomatoes, cucumbers, zucchini, basil, and fairytale eggplants abound. Most important, as Sonoma has so many wineries (grapes are a monocrop here), they grow an abundance of flowers to attract bees and hummingbirds and helpful bugs.

Bottom: This is the first scenic view guests see when they arrive at the living area of the house.

TANKLESS OR ON-DEMAND HOT WATER

The average household uses about sixty-four gallons of water each day, with water heaters the second largest household consumer of energy. A good energy-saving solution is a tankless water heater (also known as an on-demand or instantaneous water heater), which saves on space and energy. A tankless water heater provides hot water only when it is required. It does not have a storage tank, which uses energy continuously to heat water even when it's not being used. With an on-demand water heater, cold water circulates through a series of coils, which are directly heated by gas burners or electric coils; the water is heated only when there is demand.

These units provide hot water at a rate of two to five gallons per minute, depending on the model and the temperature of the groundwater. Gas-fired, on-demand water heaters produce higher flow rates than electric ones; however, they are physically larger than electric tankless units, requiring gas supply lines and sometimes more expensive venting. Some units provide enough hot water for only a tub or washing machine at one time; others can supply enough for multiple simultaneous needs. A second unit may be required if the family's hot water demands are great. These generally cost more than a typical forty-gallon water heater, but usually have longer warranties, last longer, and save the homeowner money overall in more temperate areas of the country.

Energy savings vary depending on the efficiency rating of the unit and the cost of energy in the area. When considering purchasing a water heater the homeowner needs to consider the size of the heater that will be required, installation costs, the type of fuel, and the actual size and bulkiness of the heater itself. The other issues are the flow rate of the unit and the noise level it might make. Today there are units that have smart home integration features to activate the recirculation system, set a favorite temperature, and allow for multiple on/off recirculation periods during the day through built-in timers and schedules.

LITTLE BLACK HOUSE

SITE BUILT

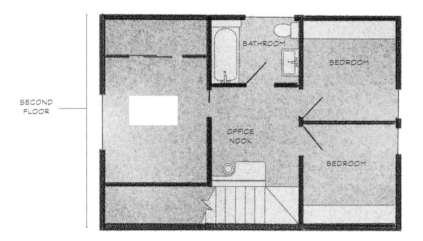

SECOND FLOOR

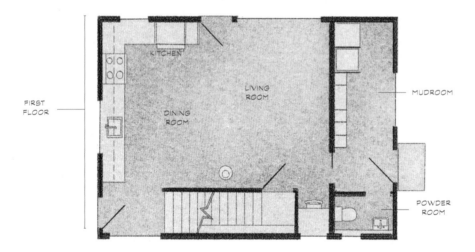

FIRST FLOOR

PHOTOGRAPHER
Susan Teare Photography
www.susanteare.com

ARCHITECT
Elizabeth Herrmann Architects
www.eharchitect.com

GENERAL CONTRACTOR
Red House Building
www.redhousebuilding.com

SIZE
1,120 square feet

LOCATION
North Fayston, Vermont

Opposite: The siding of the house is stained Western red cedar and the roofing is standing seam metal. Both materials are ideal for creating a low maintenance house although the cedar needs staining every few years. Since quality is important to them, the couple is willing to put in some maintenance to attain it.

After living in Waterbury Center for ten years, Mandy and Chad decided to build their new home in the Mad River Valley. They were drawn to its beautiful, quiet countryside and low-key vibe, combined with easy access to world-class outdoor fun such as snowboarding, skiing, biking, hiking, and paddling. With good friends living in the area and the public high school close by, it seemed like a great fit.

GREEN FEATURES
- Large deck for expanded seasonal living
- Locally sourced materials

ENERGY FEATURES
- High performance doors
- Triple-pane windows
- Daylighting
- Air-source heat pump
- Heat recovery ventilator
- Small woodstove
- Ventless heat pump dryer
- Electric hybrid heat pump water heater
- Multiple insulation layers
- LED lights

CERTIFICATION
- Efficiency Vermont Certified (for Excellence in Energy-Efficient Design and Construction) www.efficiencyvermont.com

Mandy and Chad had a clear vision of what they wanted for their new home. Energy efficiency was a priority along with an open and light-filled space. They wanted a small (but not tiny) house with all the rooms and accommodations of a larger home but without the wasted areas. They liked the modern rural barn design built with natural, high-quality materials. They also wanted to take advantage of the beautiful site, creating access to outdoor living space and maximizing views.

Above: The countertops in the kitchen are exposed edge plywood with laminate tops and the cabinets are painted white. The narrow black backsplash adds just a small pop of contrast in this neutral toned kitchen.

Opposite, top: A small desk area with a window provides a workspace on the first floor.

Opposite, bottom: The large windows provide not only beautiful views to the open meadow beyond, but also allow for natural daylighting and ventilation. The many large windows throughout their home make it feel much more spacious and comfortable—especially the large wall of glass in the living area.

SELECTING AN ARCHITECT

While reviewing architect Elizabeth Herrmann's portfolio, the couple saw a gorgeous very small home (*Micro Home*, page 102). Her design aesthetic, her expertise at designing small houses, and her very efficient use of the space made her the perfect person to take on this project.

According to Herrmann, "From the start, it was established that finish quality, good design, and high performance would not be sacrificed to satisfy budget constraints, and so the house evolved ever smaller, eliminating every inch of waste in order to meet project goals. The final plan is an unusually small house for a family of four, challenging conventional notions of size and redefining affordable design."

A WORKING DESIGN

Although this house is small for a family or four, a dog, and a cat, Herrmann provided all of the living spaces required by the family. There are three bedrooms, one and a half bathrooms, an ample kitchen for such a small house, a mud room, and several work spaces for the couple and their kids. Since they need room for just laptops and phones, Chad works at the desk on the landing while Mandy sets up on the dining table. They expect to go back to their offices more often after the pandemic, but they both feel they have adequate space to work at home. Their high schooler works in the bedroom or spreads out on the dining room table. They say the space works well for everyone.

Top, left: This small woodstove, along with an air-source heat pump, provides all the necessary heat during the colder months.

Above: There are three bedrooms, all with lots of glazing for natural lighting and ventilation.

Left: A small powder room with a petite sink and mirror is tucked away on the first floor.

MULTIPLE REASONS TO BUILD SMALL

The decision to build small was quite deliberate—Chad says he was drawn to living smaller for many years. As a bag designer, he says it's all about "deliberate, efficient, functional design. Bags require a space for everything with proper protection and easy access to those things, requiring a well-integrated, thoughtful, uncluttered appearance. I guess I wanted to make a house like a backpack."

In addition, over the years the family has spent many vacations at lakeside cabins that were small, simple structures. The family felt comfortable in those smaller spaces and appreciated the calm and simplicity of that time spent living with all the comforts you need and nothing extra. They often said, "We could live this way forever."

Although the family's Waterbury Center home, at 1,800 square feet, was not big, Chad was bothered by the wasted space, which made it possible to accumulate stuff they did not need. They decided that building a smaller home would force them to be much more deliberate and discerning about what they bought and "to only have things we need and love and to periodically get rid of things."

Chad and Mandy both lost parents shortly before they embarked on their house project. Their parents had large homes full of stuff that, after the estate sales, was dispatched to second-hand stores, recyclers, and a dumpster. They quickly realized that, other than a few exceptionally timeless or precious objects, "in the end your stuff is just . . . stuff." This also had an influence on their decision to collect less.

With one child in college and the other in high school, the couple realized they would soon be empty nesters with only Cosmo, the dog, and Pedro, the cat, for company. Building small made sense to them for their future lifestyle, and they were happy to already have downsized.

In addition, building smaller cost less money—for the build, utilities, maintenance, and home purchases. And above all they feel building smaller is responsible, using fewer resources and energy to build and run the home.

Above: Chad built a simple Baltic birch plywood desk to fit on the upstairs landing which was designed to be a work zone. He cut away a portion of the desktop to fit around the woodstove pipe that comes up from the first floor. He says the heat from the stovepipe keeps him cozy while working.

Above: A large deck permits dining and living experiences to spill outdoors, doubling the downstairs living area during warmer months. Mandy says, "Being able to use the outside as additional living and entertaining space is a critical component of living in a smaller home."

ENERGY EFFICIENCY AS A PRIORITY

The couple consulted with Efficiency Vermont on the building envelope and systems, which they found extremely helpful. All of the systems in the house were selected with energy efficiency in mind from the triple-pane windows to the multiple types of insulation used on the basement and upper floors. They avoided the use of fossil fuels with an all-electric (and wood) house. The heat recovery ventilator keeps this tightly insulated house comfortable and healthy with the continuous exchange of air.

Although the couple chose to build small, they did not skimp on quality or efficiency. Corners were not cut, and they witnessed the care and consideration put into the creation and construction. They experience beautiful views from every room and in every direction and find their home to be a calming and peaceful space. The scale perfectly balances cozy and efficient without ever feeling confined: they consider it a haven.

VENTLESS HEAT PUMP DRYERS

Ventless dryers have been popular in Europe for many years but have not been as common in the United States. One of the major disadvantages of the more commonly used vented dryers is that they take climate-controlled air from the home and pump it out of the house, making the heating and cooling system work harder to maintain a comfortable temperature.

Ventless heat pump dryers take far less air out of the house, functioning like a heat pump, recirculating hot air in the drum, and removing moisture by evaporation. Instead of the moisture being vented outside, it goes into an easily accessible compartment or passes into the home drainage system.

The average ventless unit uses far less energy than a vented model. In addition, it is more energy efficient because there isn't an opening in the outer wall, which can also be a vehicle for heat loss. Being ventless means the dryer can be located almost anywhere in the house where there is an outlet. Because it doesn't get as hot as a typical vented dryer, it is gentler on fabrics. On the downside, the cycle time may be longer, clothes do not come out feeling warm, as with a vented dryer, and it may be more expensive to buy than a vented model, although less expensive in long-term energy savings. Many of these dryers come in smaller sizes, which makes them particularly ideal for smaller houses.

BUTTERFLY GARDEN COTTAGE

SITE BUILT

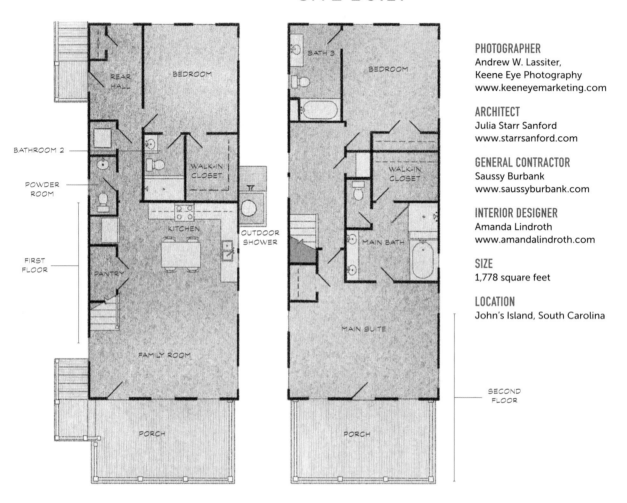

PHOTOGRAPHER
Andrew W. Lassiter,
Keene Eye Photography
www.keeneyemarketing.com

ARCHITECT
Julia Starr Sanford
www.starrsanford.com

GENERAL CONTRACTOR
Saussy Burbank
www.saussyburbank.com

INTERIOR DESIGNER
Amanda Lindroth
www.amandalindroth.com

SIZE
1,778 square feet

LOCATION
John's Island, South Carolina

Opposite: The exterior of the house is whitewashed like all houses in this area. The multiple porches make it particularly friendly to passers-by. A large oak tree in the front of the house offers some respite from the hot sun.

Gracie and Carter Redd say they love living in this Kiawah River community for many reasons. The community offers them the opportunity to live in a new waterfront location just twenty miles from historic Charleston. They can embrace an authentic Lowcountry sea islands lifestyle centered on outdoor pursuits, while enjoying twenty miles of shoreline and 2,000 acres of picturesque land. This location promotes their physical and emotional well-being amid the rejuvenating and tranquil sea islands. They like being immersed in this landscape that is home to diverse wildlife and thriving waterways.

GREEN FEATURES

- Low-flow faucets
- Multiple outdoor spaces
- Metal roof with recycled material
- WaterSense fixtures

ENERGY FEATURES

- High efficiency HVAC system
- Ceiling fans
- Dutch door
- Bahama shutters
- Tankless water heater

Above: The open floor plan on the first floor allows for easy communication between the kitchen and seating area. The ceiling fan and Dutch door offer natural ventilation for the open space.

THEY LOVE THEIR COMMUNITY

The Kiawah River's master plan and amenities were designed by world-renowned teams specializing in new urbanism and sustainable design. With a multitude of planned and natural amenities—a riverfront lodge, fitness center, stores, eateries, boat ramps and docks, indoor and outdoor events, the 75-acre Great Salt Pond, sports fields and camping structures, hiking trails, gathering areas, farms, creeks, and marshlands—it is an ideal lifestyle for them.

LIVING IN AN AGRIHOOD

Like all agrihoods (see sidebar on page 101), Kiawah River incorporates agriculture into its residential neighborhood to help foster connections between residents and local growers and producers. Kiawah River Farm, the community's working farm partnership with local farmers, features three working farms, a goat dairy, heirloom beef cattle, flower fields, beehives, and a community supported agriculture (CSA) program. The CSA offers a subscription for residents to receive weekly deliveries from the harvests of on-site farms, as well as recipes containing the latest goods and produce.

As an agrihood, Kiawah River promotes the physical and mental well-being of its residents through farm-to-table culinary experiences, educational opportunities, and outdoor living, with half of the 2,000 acres remaining undeveloped and offering an extensive network of natural trails and outdoor space for exploration and community gathering. The agrihood facilitates community food production while simultaneously providing recreation for members of the community, such as their goat yoga at the Goatery.

Below right: Gracie and Carter love the openness of their cozy kitchen that they and friends all crowd around no matter who is prepping the evening's dinner. They painted the cabinets robin's-egg blue to match their Dutch door and to add a pop of color to the mostly muted area.

Bottom: The main bedroom on the second floor has a seating area and a door leading out to a relaxing porch.

Top: The upper porch outside the main bedroom is a great place to relax and enjoy a morning coffee.

Bottom: The front porch provides a second dining area and entertaining space, along with a recreation space for Sallie, the dog.

LIVING IN JACK ISLAND VILLAGE

Gracie and Carter live in Jack Island Village, one of the neighborhoods within the Kiawah River Community. The architectural code for this area requires all home exteriors to be white, but allows for accents of color on doors, shutters, window sashes, porches, and roofs. A fundamental design feature of the houses in the village is that the porches and ornamentation need to make each home façade pleasing to neighbors passing by. The size of the houses varies, making the community more interesting. The area includes quaint, charming cottages of 800 square feet to grander custom homes, some reaching 5,556 square feet.

Top: The green Bahama shutters at the rear of the house let in cooling winds while blocking the sun.

Bottom: All the houses in the community are white and include porches so neighbors can interact when passing by.

GRACIE AND CARTER'S PIECE OF HEAVEN

Gracie and Carter's house was built on spec, so the house was completed prior to their purchase. They did have the opportunity to make cosmetic alterations to soften the look of the house, which was important to their family. Gracie and her interior designer, Amanda Lindroth, collaborated on adding pops of color to complement the coastal interiors, such as painting the kitchen cabinets robin's-egg blue to match their Dutch door. The home's can ceiling lights are not used, since the owners prefer indirect lighting via floor and table lamps and candlelit hurricane lanterns. The flooring, to their delight, is a practically indestructible manufactured hickory wood that is effortless to keep clean and coordinates well with the natural sea grass rugs they have in many locations.

They added classic Bahama shutters for privacy and solar shading. Historically, these would be mahogany, however, the couple chose aluminum for durability and a light green color to match the new shoots of spartina grass that emerge on the river and marsh each spring. The fixed louvers or blades keep out the hot sun yet allow cool trade winds to pass through to the rear bedrooms.

The couple say they love the outdoor shower, which any house on the coast or in the south must have. Their shower happens to be closest to the hot water heater, so "it's heavenly and never runs out." They also adore their stacked double porches that are deep enough to entertain. Since they are "blessed" with abundant shading from the surrounding grand oak trees, they refer to their house as a "tree house." They say that since the house is small, it is effortless to maintain. "It never feels like a burden but rather a wonderful respite."

"What we love most is our home's location within Kiawah River's Jack Island Village and how it makes engaging with close neighborhood friends so easy-breezy."

Left: This recreational area located in the Jack Island Village is available to residents for gatherings and cookouts.

DUTCH DOORS
(ALSO CALLED SPLIT DOORS
OR DOUBLE-HUNG DOORS)

Dutch doors are horizontally split in the middle so that the bottom half can remain closed while the top half is open. This configuration prevents pets or small children from leaving, as well as keeps animals from coming in. These doors also help provide natural ventilation and daylighting. In addition to the practical advantages of Dutch doors, they add character to the house. They originated in the Netherlands in the seventeenth century and were originally used to keep the farm animals from entering. Dutch doors are also available for the interior and can function as baby gates. The only disadvantages to these doors is that they are more expensive and there is additional cost for hardware and extra weathertight sealing between the halves. They come in a variety of colors and styles from varied window and door manufacturers.

Because Gracie and Carter are not fond of central air-conditioning unless absolutely necessary, they prefer the magic of cross ventilation. "We celebrate when windows are raised and the top of our Dutch door is wide open, encouraging fresh breezes throughout, which is so easy as our cottage is tiny." Often though, the lower half of the door is left open so Sallie, their dog, can meander in and out.

The robin's-egg blue Dutch door is the main entrance to the house from the front porch.

ROME DRIVE HOME

POST AND BEAM/RENOVATION

PHOTOGRAPHER
Eric Staudenmaier
www.ericstaudenmaier.com, unless
otherwise noted

ARCHITECT
ORA Architect & Design, www.ora.la

GENERAL CONTRACTOR
Moss Building Corporation

STRUCTURAL ENGINEER
Bruce Gibbons, Thornton Tomasetti
www.thorntontomasetti.com

SIZE
880 square feet (main) and 400 square
feet (ADU)

LOCATION
Los Angeles, California

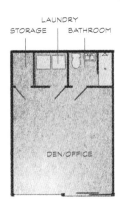

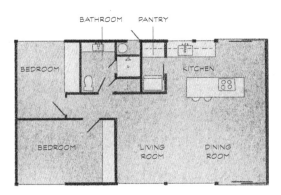

Architect Oonagh Ryan and her husband, chef Marcus Baird, were not planning to move until a friend showed them this property that was almost an acre in size. Initially they thought they would subdivide the land, build a new larger home, and rent out the current house. But upon seeing the house, they fell in love with it and decided to move in instead. They appreciate the open space and abundant wildlife around the home so much, they say they would never build a larger house.

The house is 880 square feet, originally built with post and beam construction in 1953. Oonagh says the original house had good bones with many of its original features still intact, but it was in need of updating. The home's simple, unassuming finishes were appealing. "The goal of the renovation was to capture the spirit of the original home. The design evolved in response to how the house adjusted to the seasons."

Above: The front of the house is almost all glass, with stunning views of the surrounding foliage. Deep overhangs protect the house from the elements as well as from overheating in the warmer months.

GREEN FEATURES

- Low-flow toilets (0.9 gallons per flush)
- Low-flow faucets and shower heads (1.5 gallons per minute)
- Reused original building materials

ENERGY FEATURES

- Optimal solar orientation
- Deep overhangs
- Concrete floors for thermal mass
- LED fixtures
- Cool roof
- ENERGY STAR appliances
- HVAC with high SEER rating
- Tankless hot water heater
- Passive cooling ventilation panels

Above: The kitchen, living room, and dining room are all open to each other, providing excellent air flow and space for interaction. The countertop and toe kick are brushed stainless steel.

PUTTING OFF RENOVATIONS

Oonagh and Marcus made a decision to not do renovations for a year to see how the house "behaved" throughout the year, as the seasons changed. When they initially moved in, they thought they would need a larger home and they developed a design with an addition. However, over time they realized the house was the perfect size for a couple, since the ADU (accessory dwelling unit) could always function as a guesthouse. They decided against enlarging the home and instead refocused on upgrading the existing space. Living in the house for a year also made them realize the house did not need air-conditioning and would require minimal heating since it was sited for optimum solar orientation and prevailing winds. The overhangs were the correct depth for solar control in the summer and solar gain in the winter. In the winter, the sun penetrates deep into the house, heating up the concrete slab flooring, which radiates the heat back into the space long after the sun has gone down.

The couple always intended to renovate the house. Although it was basically in good shape, the house had had little done to it since it was built and needed a lot of deferred maintenance. The couple was interested in upgrading and restoring the home's original architectural details but wanted to bring it into this century and make it feel more contemporary. Since Marcus is a chef and they entertain often, opening up the kitchen to the living and dining areas was key for them. As an architect, Oonagh believes it is important to be forward thinking in remodeling, while taking inspiration from the past life of a house. This house was a progressive modern design when originally built and she felt the home's unknown original architect would not have wanted them to be stuck in the past.

Right: The dining table and chairs are vintage Paul McCobb, Calvin Group from the 1960s. The couple found them at Hedge, a wonderful vintage store in Palm Springs. The pendant is a vintage George Nelson bubble lamp that came with the house.

Below: With the kitchen as the focal point of the living space, care was taken to create a design that did not overwhelm the space. A new island serves as the main inside gathering area. Open plywood shelves float in front of frameless glass, enhancing garden vistas and providing a display for the owner's ceramic collections. Vent panels can be seen above the windows in the kitchen.

RENOVATING OVER TIME

The renovation of the house was completed over a number of years, with long breaks in between as they saved money to fund the next project. Oonagh says, "It will never be completely done as we'll likely continue to make improvements to it every few years." Between 2009 and 2020, the couple upgraded the infrastructure (sewer, power, gas), remodeled the kitchen, put on a new roof and skylights, remodeled the bathroom and ADU, painted the house, and redid the garden, patio, and arbor, in addition to many more small tweaks to the house.

Top, left: This second bedroom serves as a home office for the couple. They don't need the bedroom for guests since they have an ADU (accessory dwelling unit). Oonagh says, "It has been a godsend to have a permanent office that's set up for work during the pandemic."

Top, right: The main bedroom benefits from a large glass window at the foot of the bed. Facing southeast, it has sunrise views over the city beyond.

Left: The outdoor area adds additional living space in the front and rear of the house. The home's connections to the garden are a daily source of joy. "Waking up to expanded views of nature in our garden and the valley below is something that never gets old."

CHOOSING PASSIVE HEATING AND COOLING

A series of wall-mounted air-conditioning units in the original house had destroyed the character of the home. Because there was no attic or crawl space, installing ducted air-conditioning to the house would have been difficult without it being exposed. Oonagh and Marcus decided instead to live without air-conditioning, leaving the existing ventilation panels in place, which provide adequate passive cooling. The vent panels, which were part of the original house, are hinged plywood panels with insect screens, located above each window in the home. They are a low-tech passive cooling system that are flipped open in spring and then closed in early winter. The cool sea breeze from the bay flows through the vent panels, pulling the hot air out of the structure on the opposite side of the house. The couple says the house is surprisingly temperate given how much glazing it has.

The home was transformed during the renovations into an airy, light-filled space by removing a wall separating the kitchen from the main space and enlarging an existing window in the kitchen. This also strengthened the connections between the living spaces and the garden outside.

Above: A new skylight in the serene bathroom fills the space with natural light. A blue plywood and laminate vanity floats over the polished concrete floor and plays off the existing neutral house finishes. Tile colors were selected to visually enlarge the small space.

Left: The interior walls of the original house (shown) impeded the transfer of light and ventilation. (Photo courtesy of the owners.)

Above: The ADU, approximately 400 square feet, used to be a two-car garage. It was already converted when the couple purchased the home; they just remodeled it to upgrade the bathroom, laundry, and infrastructure. It has served a variety of purposes over the years. The flexible space provides a quiet getaway as it opens into a shady part of the garden. It is a den where Marcus watches sports and listens to loud punk music. It is where Oonagh's architecture practice started, and during the pandemic it became Marcus's home office. It is also a guesthouse.

AN INFLUENCE ON OONAGH'S PRACTICE

From the experience renovating her own house, Oonagh says she learned that less is more if a home is thoughtfully designed. "You can live very well in smaller spaces, have less, and be happier. This house forces us to have only things we use, to live lightly, and to use our resources well." She has become a big advocate of passive design when designing for her clients, as it is the most cost-effective way to build sustainably. She also discovered the importance of outdoor spaces to wellbeing, especially during the pandemic when she and Marcus were at home all the time. The views, daylight, and strong connections to nature made for a better living environment. She comments, "A home should not be too precious; it should be comfortable, livable, and bring you joy. My favorite things about the house are its simplicity, functionality, and flexibility—there's nothing more in this home that is needed for us to live well."

POST AND BEAM

Post and beam is a very traditional type of construction using heavy timbers or engineered wood, rather than the dimensional wood (such as 2 × 4s) used for traditional framing. Timber frames and post and beam houses have been constructed for hundreds of years—in earlier times with axes, chisels, and other hand tools. Today most frames are prefabricated in a factory, and the parts are numbered and put together on-site. Unlike timber frames, which use mortise and tenon joinery and are secured with wood pegs, post and beam structures may have exposed metal fasteners or other joinery. Carefully measured, cut, and joined, they create a strong, tight frame for homes, barns, or other structures. Frames are sometimes hidden behind finished walls but are often kept visible in the interior of the house to show off the craftsmanship and to provide a warm, interesting design feature. These frames are capable of bearing heavy weight and so do not require as many vertical support posts and bearing walls as used in traditional construction. This creates a much more flexible floor plan. At the end of the life cycle of the home, these posts and beams can also be reused for other purposes.

M'S HOUSE

SITE BUILT

PHOTOGRAPHER
David Paul Bayles
www.davidpaulbayles.com, unless
otherwise noted

ARCHITECT
Studio.e Architecture
www.studioearchitecture.com

BUILDER
Stonewood Construction
www.stonewoodconstruction.com

STRUCTURAL ENGINEER
Mortier Ang Engineers
www.mortierang.com

LANDSCAPE ARCHITECTURE
Lovinger Robertson Landscape Architects
www.lovingerrobertson.com

SIZE
1,268 square feet

LOCATION
Eugene, Oregon

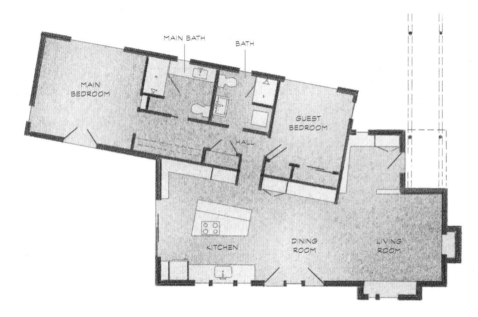

Melinda Bruce was looking to downsize from the home she had lived in for thirty years. She wanted a small, single-story, forever-designed home. It had to have open interiors that afforded lots of light, plenty of wall space for her artwork, and a kitchen large enough to indulge her love of cooking and entertaining. Vast space was less important than comfort and good design.

Above: The exterior of the house has fiber cement siding, which is long lasting and low maintenance. (Photo courtesy of Aaron Montoya, www.themontoyacollective.com.)

GREEN FEATURES

- Stormwater filtration planter
- Highly durable fiber cement siding
- Low-flow faucets and shower
- Siding installed as a ventilated rainscreen to promote durability of the building envelope

ENERGY FEATURES

- Multiple insulation layers on walls, roof, and floor
- Heat recovery ventilator
- High-efficiency ductless mini-split heat pump
- On-demand gas water heater
- ENERGY STAR appliances
- LED lighting
- Large window overhangs

FINDING JUST THE RIGHT PLACE TO LIVE

Bruce was unable to find just the right place until she came across a new townhouse development under construction in a neighborhood near her home. She liked the design and neighborhood although she didn't want a townhouse or a multistory home. She approached the on-site contractor and told him what she was looking for. He and his development partners were in negotiation on a nearby property that would accommodate three small, single-family houses adjacent to another of their townhouse projects. That sounded exactly what Bruce was looking for. When the lots were available, she purchased the middle lot which looked onto, but was not a part of, the townhouse common area. This location was ideal because she wanted to be in a developed area where she would not be isolated. She asked Jan Fillinger, a principal architect at Studio.e Architecture working on the two developments, to design her home. He designed the house to be compatible with the nearby townhouses and offered Bruce the opportunity to be part of that community.

Opposite: The open space has a multitude of windows and doors for natural lighting and ventilation. The fireplace is a modern gas inset.

Right: The bathroom combines affordable IKEA casework with a solid surface countertop and LED sconce lights for a clean and modern aesthetic.

Below: The house is open concept with all the living areas open to each other, allowing the transfer of heat and ventilation. The flooring is highly sustainable stranded bamboo engineered hardwood.

DESIGNED TO MEET HER REQUIREMENTS

Fillinger says Bruce was clearly dedicated to creating a house that was compact, right-sized, age-in-place accessible, while also embodying a sophisticated, modern, highly functional design.

With Fillinger's open concept, clean, simple, uncluttered plan, Bruce says her house feels very roomy. The large windows and sliding doors that open onto views of the trees and flower beds on her property, along with vistas of outdoor areas well beyond her lot, make her home seem much larger. After living for thirty-plus years on a large, heavily wooded lot, she now enjoys being able to have a small vegetable and flower garden. According to Fillinger, "Melinda's home is evidence that careful and deliberate design is more important than square footage for creating interior and exterior living spaces that are spacious, airy, and light filled."

Left: The rear of the house provides a good-size patio for relaxing and entertaining. Overhangs above the large sliding doors offer respite from the hot summer sun but, with the appropriate angle, allow in winter solar heating. (Photo courtesy of Aaron Montoya, www.themontoyacollective.com.)

Above: The homeowner liked the idea of being a part of a community although hers is a private house and the others are townhouses. The rear of her house is just beyond the Arcadia shared garden. (Photo courtesy of Rick Keating, www.rickkeatingphotographer.com.)

Opposite: In spite of the small square footage of the house, the kitchen is spacious and light filled. The countertops are solid surface (see sidebar), and the cabinets are custom-laminated birch.

ENERGY EFFICIENCY AS A PRIORITY

Because energy efficiency was a priority, Bruce left all decisions in that area to Fillinger, who is known not only for his beautiful designs, but also his commitment to energy efficiency. The house was built with multiple layers of insulation—blown-in fiberglass for greater thermal protection and airtightness and continuous exterior foam-board insulation added to the outside of the stud walls and the roof framing—for better-than-code energy efficiency.

In addition, there is a tankless on-demand water heater and a high-efficiency ductless mini-split heat pump to save on energy. A heat-recovery ventilation system (HRV) (see sidebar on page 59) was installed to ensure healthy indoor air and conserve the heating and cooling already created in the house.

Bruce says her home far exceeds the expectations she had when she began planning for it six years prior. "It is perfect for me in every way. It fits my aesthetic and the way I like to live now and how I want to live going forward."

SOLID SURFACE COUNTERTOPS

Solid surface is one of the most common materials used for countertops. This category was first established with Dupont's Corian, but there are now several other companies that also produce solid surface materials. These products are usually made from layers of fused acrylic, with each company having its own formulas.

There are several advantages to using solid surface: the seams are almost invisible, and it is less expensive than quartz or slab granite, but with a similar stone appearance. Mold, mildew, and bacteria cannot penetrate the nonporous surface; therefore, there is no need to apply sealants. Solid surface can also be molded into a variety of shapes for curved walls, rounded columns, and so on. This material is solid all the way through, so light scratches are almost undetectable and edges are far more durable. Plus, it is stain resistant and incredibly easy to clean. In the rare instance of surface damage, repairs are quick and easy. However, solid surface can scorch and scratch. It comes in a variety of thicknesses, with the thicker slabs being understandably more expensive and durable than the thinner ones. The solid surface used for Bruce's home is LivingStone.

THE SCOTT HOUSE

PANELIZED

PHOTOGRAPHER
Jim Miller, unless otherwise noted

ARCHITECT
Richard Pedranti Architect
www.richardpedranti.com

GENERAL CONTRACTOR
Homeowner

MANUFACTURER
Ecocor, www.ecocor.us

SIZE
1,740 square feet

LOCATION
Altamont, New York

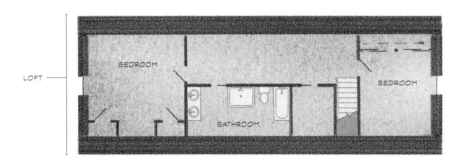

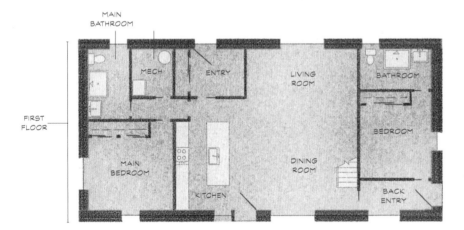

Having grown up in her family's post and beam passive solar home, Beth knew that when it was time to build her own house, it also had to be passive solar.

When Beth was little, her parents told her where on their property she should build her house, and that is where her home ended up. The house is on the highest spot on the property, adjacent to a preserve, which makes the lot feel bigger than its 8.7 acres. It is also close to her parent's home, so she can help them with yard work and other chores as they get older.

GREEN FEATURES
- Energy recovery ventilator (ERV)
- Recyclable metal roof
- Locally sourced materials
- Recycled materials
- Quartz countertops

ENERGY FEATURES
- Concrete floors
- High-efficiency windows and doors
- Super-insulated foundation
- Super-insulated wall panels
- Optimal solar orientation

ENERGY EFFICIENCY AS A PRIORITY

Beth's major priority was to build an energy efficient house, while taking advantage of the latest building science. "With the future uncertain in terms of climate and weather conditions, it's nice to know that even without power, the temperature in my house won't go much under 60 or over 80, and I'll be able to heat and cool it without spending very much money." Keeping the house smaller than a typical built home will also reduce its environmental footprint.

After being deeded the lot, Beth waited several years to build the house until she felt passive house technology had developed enough to allow her to build the house to the high standards she wanted. (When the house was completed, she was convinced that the wait had been worthwhile.) She opted not to have the house certified by Passive House (PH), although it meets and exceeds their standards.

CHOOSING AN ARCHITECT AND MANUFACTURER

Building the house with prefabrication technology was also on Beth's agenda. "I really believe that this is the best, most efficient way to build. I like that it reduces the construction time on sites and reduces waste." Ecocor was the perfect solution for Beth's building goals because they build prefabricated structures to Passive House standards. Chris Corson, the owner of Ecocor, worked closely with Beth to manufacture her highly efficient panelized system (see sidebar on page 27).

Architect Richard Pedranti had designed a series of plans for Ecocor. Beth says his designs matched her desire for a minimalist Scandinavian look and already had many of her must-haves. Pedranti was great at adapting the plans to her wishes. She added a second story and the potential for up to two additional bedrooms in that space. Pedranti won a 2020 AIA Pennsylvania merit award for this design.

Beth wanted smaller bedrooms and bathrooms than are typical, with a large open space in the center of the house. The layout was to have a bedroom and bathroom at each end of the house with a large open living space in between. She desired an exterior door near each bedroom, which is smart for safety as well as for easily stepping into the outdoors.

Opposite: Beth loves the polished interior concrete floor with some exposed aggregate (the little stones that are mixed in the concrete), which she says makes it interesting and natural looking. "You would think concrete would be cold, but it's often warm where the sun hits it or just room temperature. It's very durable and doesn't seem to stain or show dirt.

Above: The kitchen has an abundance of storage space including in the front of the island where she put large red oak plywood drawers. The island has quartz countertops. Beth used a watered-down white paint mixture to give the exposed ceiling framing on the first floor a whitewashed look. (Photo courtesy of Christian Corson.)

Left: Beth put together the large, live-edge oak dining table from a slab that she sanded and finished and to which she added metal legs. The wood is red oak, a very common local tree.

WORKING AS A GENERAL CONTRACTOR AND MORE

Beth was very involved in the process of building the house, which meant that she had to learn a great deal about construction very quickly. She ended up doing many tasks herself when there were no local experts available. She believes that in the future, as Passive House standards become more mainstream in this country, it will be easier to find knowledgeable craftsmen to build these types of homes. Beth recommends that anyone considering building a Passive House should first find out whether or not there are local people capable of building to this standard.

Beth designed and constructed most of the IKEA kitchen herself. She admits it was a little scary to design it herself and she feared she would do something she would later regret, but now she wouldn't change anything. The kitchen is one of her favorite parts of the house, with more storage space than she can currently use, and the quartz counter on the island is so large she can have multiple cooking projects going on at once. Instead of having stools at the island, she opted for large storage drawers with fronts of red oak plywood. Beth installed some of the insulation, drywall, and trim, painted the interior of the house, and put stain on the exterior. She also installed the expensive cable railing on the steps, which was a challenge. Instead of taking the easier route of painting the wood ceiling white, Beth opted to whitewash it instead, adding warmth to the space. Although it was much more difficult, she ended up with a great result.

She admits that doing so much of the work made the construction time longer than it might have been with professionals. But she enjoyed the work and is delighted with her finished home. Remarkably, while building the house Beth was also working at her own business full-time.

Opposite: The rear of the house is south facing and has more windows than the front of the house, in order to capture solar energy. (Photo courtesy of the homeowner.)

Above: Prefab manufacturer Ecocor used a highly efficient panelized system in the construction of the house. (Photo courtesy of Christian Corson.)

FEELING BIGGER THAN ITS SQUARE FOOTAGE

With the exposed framing in the ceiling of the first floor and the vaulted ceiling on the second floor, the house feels much larger than its footprint. The windows are large enough that wherever you are in the house, you get a sense of the outdoors without feeling too exposed.

Above: To help her get through the long New York winters, Beth created a wall of plants for an outside feel. Painting the wall dark helps her living room look a little like a forest.

Right: The entrance on the east (gable) end is important because with the amount of snowfall Beth says the house gets, snow from the roof often completely covers the north and south doors. One of the things she likes is when she is working in the spare bedroom by this door, she can easily step outside and receive deliveries.

BETH LOVES THE HOUSE SHE CREATED

Beth's passive house is very quiet and feels very secure. She hears almost nothing outside, even the rain on her metal roof. "I really like how it looks from a distance when I'm walking around the field on the trails."

BLOWER DOOR TEST

A blower door test is a diagnostic tool used to measure the airtightness of a structure and to see if there are any leaks in it. A powerful fan is mounted in the frame of an exterior door. During a depressurization test, the fan pulls air out of the house, lowering the interior pressure and pulling air in from the outside through unsealed cracks and openings. A pressure gauge measures the amount of air pulled out of the house by the fan.

Results of this test can determine if there are leaks in the air sealing, which can then be amended. Properly sealing a house will increase comfort, reduce energy costs, and improve indoor air quality. This test is required for certain certification programs, including ENERGY STAR and Passive House (Passivhaus). Passive House (PH) has the most stringent blower door test requirements, allowing a maximum infiltration of 0.6 air changes per hour (ACH) when measured at 50 pascals pressure difference. (Pascals are a measure of pressure.) For reference, typical new houses will test between 4 to 6 ACH @ 50 pascals, and typical existing houses will test between 8 to 10 ACH @ 50 pascals. Results below 2.0 ACH @ 50 pascals may be considered "tight," while 1.0 ACH @ 50 pascals is a typical target for high-performance new construction. The results of the blower door test for Beth's house was 0.28 ACH @ 50 pascals, which exceeds certification requirements for Passive House. When a home is built very tight with minimal air leaks, a heat recovery ventilator (HRV) or energy recovery ventilator (ERV) (see sidebar on page 59) is generally recommended to bring fresh air into the house. These units exchange stale heated or cool air with fresh air.

BOW HILL HOUSE

STRUCTURAL INSULATED PANELS (SIPS) AND TIMBER FRAME

PHOTOGRAPHER
Lucas Henning
www.swiftphotostudio.com

ARCHITECT AND MANUFACTURER
FabCab, www.fabcab.com

GENERAL CONTRACTOR
James Hall and Associates
www.jameshallandassociates.com

INTERIOR DESIGNER
Lydia Huffman, LH Design Studio
www.mylhdesign.com
Elizabeth Davis, Ecd Design LLC

SIZE
1,835 square feet (main) and
839 square feet (ADU)

LOCATION
Bow, Washington

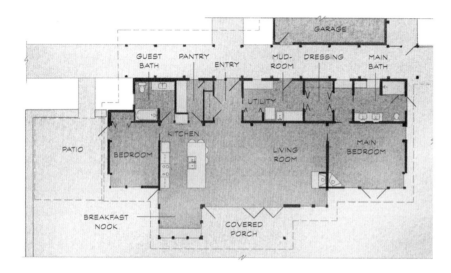

The homeowners downsized to a new home to meet their current needs and to have no wasted space. They wanted to be able to enjoy the entire house rather than have space they didn't use. This location was the perfect choice for the couple with its easy commute to Seattle, where many of their longtime friends live. They also were excited to develop these five acres of sunny property with its beautiful views. Living in the country has given them a chance to cultivate a lifestyle focused on the land with an orchard, greenhouse, vegetable garden, firepit, and boccie court, as well as multiple outdoor spaces, covered and open. It is a place their three adult children, who live in various parts of the country, love to visit.

The house was built with a generous main suite and a second bedroom, which they use as an office. As a place for family and friends to stay, an accessory dwelling unit (ADU) was added, which is easily accessible from the main house via a covered breezeway.

Above: The exterior siding is mostly fiber cement with some metal, both which require minimal maintenance. The roof is standing seam metal. The placement of the garage creates a courtyard between the house, workshop, and ADU.

GREEN FEATURES
- Metal roofing with recycled material
- Natural materials
- Fiber cement siding
- Quartz countertops

ENERGY FEATURES
- Hydronic in-floor radiant heat
- Concrete floors
- Energy recovery ventilator (ERV)
- Structural insulated panels (SIPs)
- High performance windows
- Powered blinds
- Clerestory windows

Above: Kitchen appliances are all ENERGY STAR rated and the countertops are quartz, a highly sustainable material.

BUILDING PREFAB

The couple specifically wanted to build the house with prefab construction as long as they had the flexibility to customize the house to their needs. FabCab was happy to work with the homeowners to personalize it and they designed the house to be one level for accessibility since the couple wanted this to be their forever home. The couple also wanted lots of storage, an open concept, connection to outdoors in all seasons, and accessible routes between the garage, the home, and the ADU.

Because the connection to the exterior and the beautiful views was so important, the house has a bifold door system (see sidebar on page 195) which opens most of the southwest side of the house and leads to the covered patio.

DESIGNING THE HOUSE TO FEEL LARGER

To make the house feel more spacious, the architects designed the house with an open floor plan, soaring vaulted ceilings, flexible spaces, and ample daylighting. The bifold doors vastly extend the living space with almost no separation between the interior and exterior when the doors are open. The outdoor living spaces extend the living area with several outdoor areas, such as the firepit and boccie court.

Above: The timber frame construction can be seen throughout the living area. The sweeping ceiling elevated to the rear of the house creates a more expansive space and allows for added light into the house via clerestory windows.

Below, left: Stunning Padilla Bay can be seen from the front door through the interior to the glass bifold doors on the other side of the house.

Below, right: The small breakfast nook off the kitchen is light filled with three sides of windows, and is in addition to the dining area between the kitchen and living room.

BUILDING THE HOUSE TO BE ENERGY EFFICIENT

Every effort was made to make the house as energy efficient as possible. The concrete floors add thermal mass for passive solar gain, as well as adding an aesthetically pleasing and low maintenance feature to the home. The concrete floors also do not scratch, an additional bonus since there are pets in the house. In-floor radiant heat uses less energy than many other types of systems and provides an even, comfortable heating. The mini-split units, mainly for air-conditioning, can also provide supplemental quick heat, if the radiant system is ever turned off. The energy recovery ventilator (ERV) keeps the air healthy in the house while also conserving energy.

Above: Floor-to-ceiling windows can be seen in the rear of both the house and the ADU. There are several seating areas in the exterior to expand the space of the house. The extended roofline protects the house and controls the sunlight and solar gain in both summer and winter.

Above: A covered trellis is outside the kitchen and home office. This outdoor space offers additional seating and an outdoor cooking area.

A VERY PLEASING RESULT

FabCab program manager Bruce Waltar says there were many design opportunities in planning this house that allowed for client requests such as placing the home at an elevation to capture the best sun and views. This allowed for the lower patio and bocce court to be at grade and for the creation of the breakfast nook bump-out adjacent to the five-panel bifold door system. In the end Waltar says, "It was a pleasure helping the homeowners create their retirement/forever home oriented to maximize natural light and views, featuring aging-in-place ideas, and also providing additional spaces for friends and family to enjoy the property."

GLASS BIFOLD DOOR SYSTEMS

Glass bifold door systems allow for large areas of unobstructed views, usually between the interior and exterior in the home or in commercial spaces. In some cases, they are also used as dividers between interior rooms. These can span large open areas with a hidden track system making them virtually disappear. There are also retractable bug screens that allow the owner to have the natural ventilation without being bothered by pests. The systems are available in a variety of metals, sizes, and colors. The bifold system in the Bow Hill House is by Andersen.

Above: The bifold doors open almost completely for easy access to the outdoor spaces, providing natural light and ventilation.

LITTLE RED HOUSE

RENOVATION

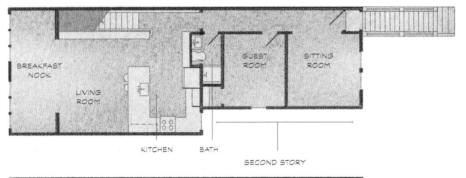

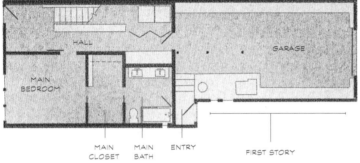

BREAKFAST NOOK

LIVING ROOM

GUEST ROOM

SITTING ROOM

KITCHEN   BATH

SECOND STORY

HALL

GARAGE

MAIN BEDROOM

MAIN CLOSET   MAIN BATH   ENTRY

FIRST STORY

PHOTOGRAPHER
Henry Gao, Red Dot Studio
www.reddotstudio.com

ARCHITECT
Red Dot Studio
www.reddotstudio.com

GENERAL CONTRACTOR
Andrew Fay, Fay Construction &
Restoration
www.fayconst.com

SIZE
1,593 square feet

LOCATION
San Francisco, California

Opposite: The front of the home retains the features and charm a Pelton Cottage is known for, which are a harmonious exterior composition and ornate trim. Their diminutive size makes them more human scale than their larger Victorian counterparts.

After living in a condo for seven years, Heather and Gene were ready for a move and hoped, optimistically, to find a home in Dogpatch, an area they had grown to love. They didn't know anything about Pelton Cottages (see sidebar on page 203), but they couldn't miss the cute row of little Victorians they would pass on their walks around town. When one of these historic homes came on the market, they went to the open house, and immediately fell in love with it. Naturally, the fact that the house was a Pelton Cottage was part of the appeal.

Heather and Gene like Dogpatch because of its proximity to downtown San Francisco with its mass transit and highways. They also like its "slightly frontier-like feeling," with an eclectic mix of historic homes, old factories, a salsa club, and small businesses. The salsa club was eventually replaced by condos, but the quirky neighborhood feeling still exists.

GREEN FEATURES

- No gas
- Ultra-low-flow toilets
- Recycled and reused materials
- Roof run-off diversion and storage
- Cellulose and natural fiber
  insulation

ENERGY FEATURES

- PV panels
- Skylight for daylighting
- Super insulation
- Induction stove
- Concrete floors
- Skylights
- Radiant heat
- Whole house energy monitor
- Electric car charger
- Solar-powered attic fan for cooling

TAKING TIME TO RENOVATE

Heather and Gene fell in love with the house as it was. Initially they installed solar panels and moved a closet, but otherwise settled in without further renovations. Over time, as they lived there, they started to see the untapped potential of their home and decided to do a more extensive renovation. They employed Red Dot Studio to design their home partly because they had designed another Pelton house on the same block. But they also felt they communicated well with Karen Curtis, the lead designer of Red Dot Studio, and believed she shared their vision for the house.

MUST-HAVES IN THEIR NEW HOME

The couple wanted a design that would make the house as energy efficient as possible. They saved money for a few years before the renovation. They did everything they could afford to reduce their carbon footprint during construction. They went all-electric because, even though gas heating is cheaper, electric was the best option for limiting their carbon footprint as more and more California energy is coming from renewables. They use an electric boiler, knowing it is less efficient than other options.

Heather and Gene extensively renovated the rear of their home and preferred a mid-century design for the renovated spaces. They opted to keep the front two rooms in their original Victorian style. Since the house was originally too dark and subject to extreme hot or cold conditions, they wanted to bring in more natural light, while reducing the temperature fluctuations, allowing more cool air to flow through the house.

Opposite: The rear wall of the kitchen is a powerhouse of storage, allowing the remainder of the cabinet space to be open to the living area. Plywood cabinets match the stair storage wall. Many appliances were reused. This is the sort of kitchen that is meant to be practical in equal parts to "pretty."

Below: The owners' love of color comes through with the deep yellow walls in this sitting area.

Right: Reclaimed San Francisco bricks form the patio in the rear yard. The owners opted for a green rear wall to complement the ongoing planting work in the garden space.

Below: The slatted storage shelves that face the main bedroom on the bottom floor match the design of the stair storage on the second floor.

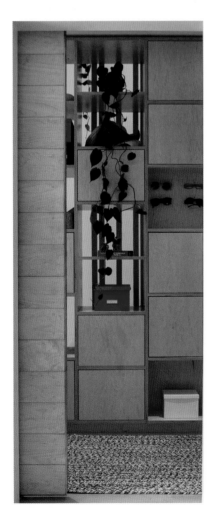

ADAPTING THE HOUSE TO WORK AT HOME

Heather and Gene both started working at home at the start of the Covid-19 pandemic. Their offices are located by the windows facing the backyard, where they "can watch the seasons change and the birds fly by." They converted what was going to be a breakfast nook into a second office space, which works out very well for them.

POSITIVE CHANGES FOR THE HOUSE

The rear of the home had previously been divided up and added onto with multiple small spaces. The bottom level of the home had not been used. The renovation knit the upstairs and downstairs spaces together. The stairs in line with the front door and signature railroad Victorian hall lead to the lower level where the main bedroom looks out on the garden. The rear of the home now opens to the peak with high ceilings and skylights to become an airy kitchen and living space with large windows overlooking the yard.

The couple appreciated the close interaction with Red Dot Studio and their contractor, both of whom kept them informed throughout the process. They also liked being able to contribute to the design process. They both feel like this house isn't small anymore even though there was no change to exterior or additional square footage added to the structure. They say, "It feels so big!" They were surprised it would be included in a book about smaller homes.

Above: The bookcase on the first floor backs up to the staircase. It is an organizing element allowing the homeowners to store and display objects. The storage wall transitions to a laundry closet, neatly tucked away under the stairs.

Below: The barrier between the living room and the stairs is a display and storage device for the owners' plants and collections.

Above and Opposite: The rear of the home had been partitioned into a series of small rooms with low ceilings. By opening to the peak and creating a living space with various nooks, the home now feels spatially large with a kitchen and living space. The skylights are positioned for daylighting.

A BELOVED HOME

The couple says they love all the natural light pouring into the rooms. The stairwell and the cubbies at the stairs allow for lots of plants to cascade down and bring life into the home. The redesign allowed them to improve the environmental footprint of their home. A rainwater capture system in the backyard helps them grow vegetables. They love their newly renovated "old" home.

PELTON COTTAGES

John Cotter Pelton, Jr. designed his "cheap dwelling" series homes in the 1880s for small families of moderate means that were published in the *San Francisco Evening Bulletin*. It was said they included so much information anyone could build from his plans without further information. His second installment in the paper was the design used for twenty-six houses in the Dogpatch neighborhood of San Francisco. These houses, each built on a 20-foot-wide lot, were four-room cottages at 772 square feet. They had flexible space so they could be personalized by the owner. Only sixteen of the Pelton Cottages are left, including this Little Red House. They have all had extensive renovations and upgrading to be brought up to current building code.

BLANCO
RIVER HOUSE

SITE BUILT

PHOTOGRAPHER
Luis Vargas
www.ayalavargas.com

ARCHITECT
Brett Zamore Design
www.brettzamoredesign.com

GENERAL CONTRACTOR
Green Guild Studio
www.greenguildstudio.com

SIZE
1,700 square feet

LOCATION
Wimberley, Texas

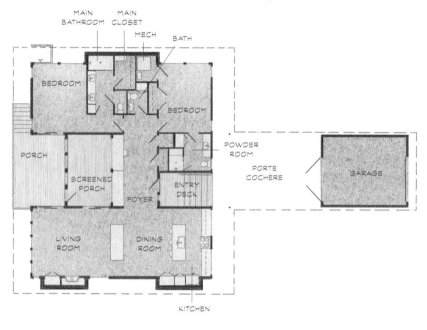

G reg Martin's parents purchased a small home in the Hill Country around 1976. His parents loved this place and over the years replaced the small deck with a larger one and converted half of the detached workshop into a guesthouse, which they often rented out for weekends. Greg has fond memories of the family reunions held there for over twenty years. Years later Greg inherited the property and it remained as it was until the great Memorial Day Flood in 2015 rendered the house and the workshop/guesthouse unlivable. It was this event that spurred him and his wife, Suzy, to demolish the old place and to rebuild it.

Above: The house has large overhangs around the periphery and larger ones over the decks to protect from rain and the sun. Siding is locally sourced natural cedar and limestone. The exterior landscape surface includes primarily crushed granite to allow for permeability.

GREEN FEATURES

- Water storage tanks
- No VOC paint
- FSC-certified plywood for cabinetry, oak flooring, and cedar siding
- Low-flow water fixtures
- Recycled materials
- Locally sourced materials
- Standing seam metal roof with recycled aluminum
- Permeable landscaping
- Raised wood floor foundation on piers
- Granite countertops

ENERGY FEATURES

- LED Lights
- ENERGY STAR rated appliances
- High efficiency furnace and air-conditioning
- Large overhangs
- High efficiency windows and doors
- Wired for PV panels

WORKING WITH AN ARCHITECT

In early 2017, Suzy saw an article about Brett Zamore Design in the *Houstonia Magazine*. The couple met with Brett, gave him a crude sketch of the kind of home they wanted, and discussed their needs and the reality of the budget. Greg is sure Zamore did the design in his head right there at that first meeting. Within a short time they had a working model for the new house and started off on their project.

The couple had a long list of must-haves for Zamore. Multiple windows facing the river was a priority. They also knew they wanted a metal roof, walk-in showers, no bathtubs, and an outdoor shower. They wanted a gas burning fireplace. A desk area in the entryway hall would be a good use of that space, they thought. They also wanted a covered deck, with half exposed to outdoors and half enclosed. A separate garage, which they now call the Barn, was also on the list. It would serve as a workshop and a place to keep equipment. They have planned for a rainwater harvesting system.

Opposite: All appliances in the kitchen are ENERGY STAR rated and the granite countertops are eco-friendly.

Left: The house has an open floor plan that, in addition to promoting easy communication in the house, also allows light and air to permeate throughout.

Below: The living room is at the rear of the house, providing the best views of the river and the other natural surroundings.

BUILDING ON A SMALL SCALE AND ENERGY EFFICIENTLY

It was important for them to build the house on a small scale, but they say the house feels quite spacious due to the open layout, high ceilings, ample skylights, and the numerous large windows. Greg says, "I'm always checking to make sure the lights aren't tuned on because so much light comes in naturally." Having a *porte cochere* (a covered entrance large enough for vehicles to pass through) connecting the house to the Barn also makes the house feel more expansive.

It was important to the couple to build the house as energy efficiently and sustainable as possible. The house uses electricity but is ready for future solar panels, all of their appliances, lighting, and HVAC equipment are low energy, and windows and doors are high efficiency.

Left: The evenly spaced operable windows of the living room face the river, providing a natural cooling effect throughout the home.

ALTERING THE PLAN TO PREPARE
FOR FUTURE STORMS

After the flood there was an elevation requirement for new construction; the finished floor is required to be a minimum of one foot above the Base Flood Elevation determined by FEMA. Ultimately, they did not build on the old house footprint; the new house is set back and upslope from the previous footprint.

The couple feel they were fortunate to have an excellent architect and builder to complete this project in such a beautiful location. They say the new house is a dream come true. They hope this house will always stay in the family.

Top, left: Sliding glass doors provide access to the rear deck from the main bedroom.

Top, right: A desk and sitting area in the hallway just beyond the entrance is good use of space. Skylights bring an abundance of light into the area.

Left One of the homeowner's must-haves was an outdoor shower, located at the rear of the house facing the Blanco River.

BUILDING ON PIERS

After the Memorial Day flood in the Houston area in 2015 the Federal Emergency Management Agency (FEMA) prepared new 100-year flood plain maps which required all new structures to be raised above the new base flood elevation (BFE). The finished floor of the family's new home is eight feet higher than the finished floor of the previous house. Building the home on piers allows the home to sit above grade and to allow any potential flood water to move without interruption under the home.

A pier foundation is constructed with vertical concrete piers and pier caps above grade that transfer the building load to the ground. Steel or wood beams are built on top of the raised pier caps which support the load of the house. Since wood absorbs carbon, Zamore chose to use pressure-treated wood as it was environmentally friendly as well as more economical.

Some designers prefer to have a continuous wall with flood vents along the lower perimeter of the home, but architect Zamore thought it was best to leave the area 100 percent open to allow the underside to breathe, with proper air flow, thus avoiding the growth of mildew and rot. This configuration allows water to naturally move under the house if a flood occurs. The raised floor on piers protects the house from potential floods, aids in cooling, and provides needed ventilation under the home. In addition, it creates a crawl space for easy access to wiring and plumbing. Zamore says this is a much more sustainable, eco-friendly method to build; concrete foundations have a larger carbon footprint than the modest concrete in the raised pier caps. This type of foundation also allows for the ground to absorb water, a big issue in urban areas where a more impermeable area equates to greater potential for flooding.

TREE HOME

SITE BUILT

PHOTOGRAPHER
Cesar Rubio
www.cesarrubio.com

ARCHITECT
Rohleder Borges Architecture
www.rb-a.net

GENERAL CONTRACTOR
Richard Hart & Co.
www.richardhartco.com

SIZE
1,098 square feet (main house),
320 square feet (ADU)

LOCATION
Cloverdale, California

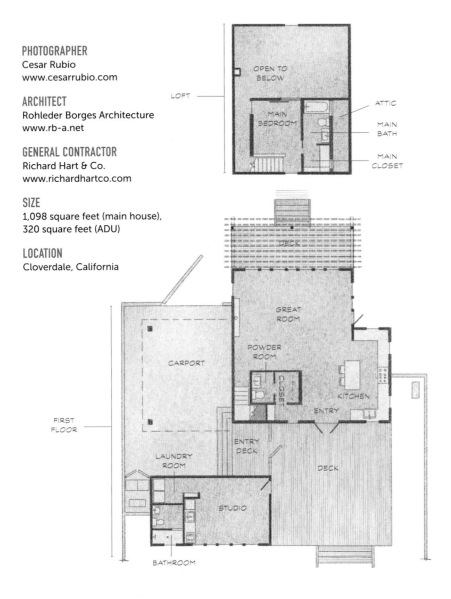

In 2013, Jenness Brewer retired and decided to move from Los Angeles to the wine country in Northern California. The area reminded her of the beautiful vineyards in Italy, which she often visited earlier in her life. In Asti, on the Russian River, four miles south of Cloverdale, Jenness renovated a 100-year-old farmhouse. She chose that house because it was big enough for her three grown daughters to be together for holidays. It was, however, not big enough for her sister to move in as well. For Jenness to get her sister to move from Seattle closer to her, she needed to build her a house in town.

Above: The rusted steel fence enclosing the property adds an element of industrial panache to the project. The fencing on the deck is cedar and will fade eventually to a light gray. Jenness also wanted the house's exterior to fit in with the other homes in this older neighborhood.

GREEN FEATURES

- Low-flow faucets and showerhead
- Reclaimed materials
- Quartz countertops

ENERGY FEATURES

- High-efficiency windows
- Mini-split heating and cooling
- Highly insulated envelope

Above: The kitchen of the small one-bedroom home was designed to be the center of daily life for Heartie Anne and her family. The space was inspired by commercial kitchens and is clutter-free, with few upper cabinets. Jenness requested there be no extra room for collecting stuff that is not needed. The island is composed of reclaimed wine barrels and the countertops are quartz.

FINDING THE PERFECT LOCATION

One day while walking her dog in the nearby town of Cloverdale, Jenness came across a lovely little cottage on a small, narrow lot. She thought the house was charming but was more impressed by the mature trees surrounding it: a large live oak, a black walnut, an olive tree, and an enormous pecan tree. She knew it would be the perfect house for her sister, Heartie Anne. Unfortunately, at the time, the house was not for sale. She often found herself in front of the small house, imagining it was hers. Two years later, a friend called to say that the house was for sale. Her friend walked through the house and told her the trees were impressive, but the house was not. Jenness wanted the house anyway. She was the highest bidder, and the place was hers.

DECIDING WHAT TO DO WITH HER NEW PURCHASE

Jenness had a local contractor look over the 1890-built house. There was no foundation, the wiring was outside the walls, and the contractor told her it had to come down. There was nothing to salvage from the house except the surrounding magnificent trees. Jenness hired architect Andrew Borges and contractor Richard Hart to build the new house, the same team she worked with for several other projects, including renovating her 100-year-old farmhouse.

Right: The dark cedar gas fireplace, reaching almost to the height of the thirty-foot ceiling, presents the house with an unexpected, impressive architectural feature. The vaulted ceiling (eighteen feet to the ridge) adds a lot of volume for the square footage, maximizing the available space.

Below: The first floor has an open floor plan and opens to the upstairs bedroom with a Juliet-type balcony.

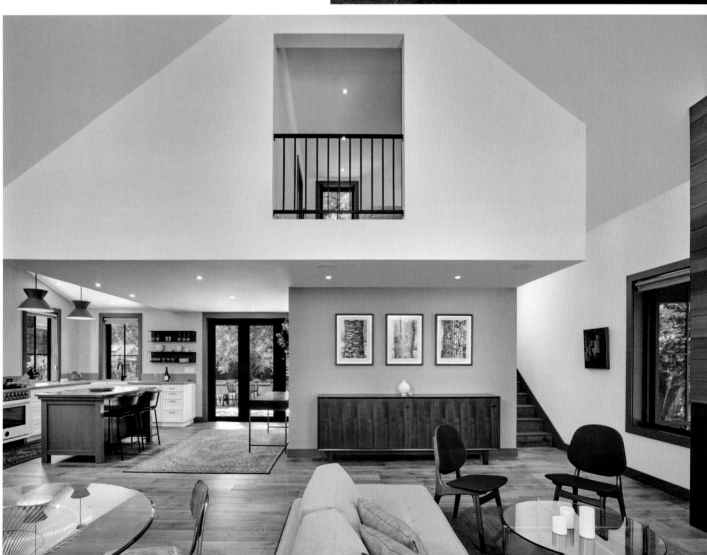

DESIGNING AND BUILDING A NEW HOUSE

Designing the house was fast, but she had to wait two years for Hart to be available to do the construction, which took fifteen months due to slowdowns caused by the Covid-19 pandemic.

Jenness knew she wanted the new house to be small, which was also necessary because of the lot's size. Her primary goal in building the house was to preserve the trees and design the structure around them. She wanted the size of the outdoor decking to be equal to the square footage of the house's interior. The exterior design of the house also had to fit in architecturally with the rest of the older neighborhood.

Because the lot was big enough for a second structure, Jenness opted to include an accessory dwelling unit (ADU). She named it the Schoolhouse, as it reminded her of a one-room, turn-of-the-century school.

Architect Borges says he particularly enjoyed working with Jenness since she was a return client, and it allowed his team to begin the design process from a place of mutual trust. "We were able to start with the client's love of symmetry, her appreciation of materiality, and her commitment to not building more than is needed." He describes the house as "a contemporary space that touches on something old and familiar."

Although energy efficiency was an important aspect of the design, it was challenging to take advantage of solar energy with the large canopy of trees surrounding the house. With the concern for efficiency, they chose highly efficient HVAC systems and windows.

Opposite: The windows of the ADU are the same as the main house, tying the two structures together.

Above: The house's porch has a post and beam gazebo, which echoes the feel of the farmhouse where Jenness lives. The decking is made of Western red cedar.

Right: The front of the ADU is fiber cement, but the sides are clad in Corten steel. This configuration makes the small studio recede from view. The materials are a nod to the building façades of the old West, where a different material was used on the front of the structure and another on the sides.

Above: Having a large outdoor space was essential to Jenness. This large deck in the rear of the house was the perfect solution.

Opposite: The upstairs bedroom has a barn door that slides open to reveal the space below. The room can be closed off for privacy or opened to the rest of the house to allow conversation and light to come through.

LIVING BIGGER IN A PETITE HOUSE

Although the house has a small footprint, Jenness says it feels like a large house with high ceilings and the many windows bringing in the outdoors. She says the house also feels exceptionally private because of the elevated front deck lifting the front structure above the street.

BARN DOORS

Barn doors are particularly beneficial in small houses because they take up less space than traditional doors that swing in and out on hinges. They are typically composed of one or two large panels hung from a heavy bar mounted above a door opening. The door moves along the bar using a set of rollers attached to the top of the frame. Often antique or reclaimed doors are repurposed as barn doors, but new doors are also available.

Barn doors can be used as entrance doors, closets, room dividers, and for less traditional purposes, such as concealing a television or storage space; in this house, it was used to open the bedroom to the lower area. Barn doors are available in various styles, from rustic to very modern, in a wide range of materials and colors. There are also space-saving pocket doors closing off the three bathrooms in the house.

SUPPLIERS

COACH HOUSE

Aculux (recessed light fixtures)
www.aculux.acuitybrands.com

Benjamin Moore (paint)
www.benjaminmoore.com

Bosch (washer and dryer)
www.bosch-home.com/us

Cambria (kitchen quartz countertops)
www.cambriausa.com

Carrier (split system heat pump)
www.carrier.com

Clipper Creek (car charger)
www.clippercreek.com

Dekton (bathroom quartz
countertops)
www.cosentino.com

Feiss (light fixtures)
www.generationlighting.com

GE (microwave)
www.geappliances.com

Loewen (front door, some windows)
www.loewen.com

Marvin (replacement windows)
www.marvin.com

Miele (refrigerator, induction cooktop,
oven, and refrigerator)
www.mieleusa.com

Rejuvenation (light fixtures)
www.rejuvenation.com

Restoration Hardware (light fixtures)
www.rh.com

Sonneman (light fixtures)
www.sonnemanawayoflight.com

Velux (skylights)
www.veluxusa.com

WAC (recessed light fixtures)
www.waclighting.com

BELLINGHAM PREFAB HOUSE

Asko (washer and dryer)
www.asko.com

Bosch (dishwasher)
www.bosch-home.com

Caesarstone (countertops)
www.caesarstoneus.com

Dacor (stovetop and oven)
www.dacor.com

Daikin (heat pump)
www.northamerica-daikin.com

Danze (touchless faucets)
www.gerber-us.com

Ecotech Solar (PV panels)
www.ecotechsolar.com

LifeBreath (HRV)
www.lifebreath.com

Montigo (fireplace)
www.montigo.com

Sharp (microwave and stove vent)
www.sharpusa.com

Sierra Pacific (windows and doors)
www.sierrapacificwindows.com

Smith & Vallee Woodworks (custom
cabinetry)
www.smithandvallee.com

Subzero (refrigerator/freezer)
www.subzero-wolf.com

BULLY HILL HOUSE

AlexAllen Studio (lights)
www.alexallenstudio.com

Badeloft (bathtub and sink)
www.badeloftusa.com

Bertazzoni (kitchen appliances)
www.us.bertazzoni.com

Big Ass Fans (fan)
www.bigassfans.com

Blue Dot (sofa)
www.bludot.com

Brizo (bathroom faucets and fixtures)
www.brizo.com

Corten Roofing
www.cortenroofing.com

Flos (lighting)
www.flos.com

IKEA (studio cabinets and shelving)
www.ikea.com/us/en

Morsø (fireplace insert)
www.morsoe.com/us

Navien (propane boiler)
www.navieninc.com

Pella Windows
www.pella.com

Tech Lighting (lights)
www.techlighting.com

Vitamin Design (dining table & stools)
www.vitamin-design.com

OAK HILL HOUSES

Benjamin Moore (paints and finishes)
www.benjaminmoore.com

Blomberg (kitchen appliances)
www.blombergappliances.com

Bradford White (hot water heaters)
www.bradfordwhite.com

Broan (range hood)
www.broan-nutone.com/en

Contech (lighting fixtures)
www.contechlighting.com

Duravit (bathroom vanity, sink, faucet,
heated and lit mirror)
www.duravit.us

Elkay (kitchen sink and faucet)
www.elkay.com/us

Hunter Panel (insulation)
www.hunterpanels.com

IKEA (cabinetry)
www.ikea.com/us/en

Kohler (bathroom fixtures)
www.us.kohler.com/us/

Master Craft (flooring)
www.themasterscraft.com

Pella (windows)
www.pella.com

Richelieu (hardware)
www.richelieu.com

Richlite (recycled paper countertops)
www.richlite.com

Robi (decking)
www.robidecking.com

Samsung (HVAC mini-splits)
www.samsung.com/us

Spore (doorbell)
www.sporedoorbells.com

Steel It (metal coating)
www.steel-it.com

Troscan Design (furniture)
www.troscandesign.com

Tubelite (glazing)
www.tubeliteinc.com

Y Lighting (pendants)
www.ylighting.com

THE LUCKI FARMHOUSE

Artemide (lights)
www.artemide.com/en/home

Daikin Altherma (heat pump & water heater)
www.daikin.com

Graypants (dining table pendant)
www.graypants.com

Grohe (faucets)
www.grohe.us

Hansgrohe (shower accessories)
www.hansgrohe-usa.com

JennAir (kitchen appliances)
www.jennair.com

Jøtul (fireplace)
www.jotul.com

Juno (lights)
www.juno.acuitybrands.com

Kohler (sink)
www.us.kohler.com/us/

Kuzco Lighting (Kitchen island pendant)
www.kuzcolighting.com

Lenova (kitchen sink)
www.lenovagroup.com

LG (washer and dryer)
www.lg.com/us/laundry

Lunos (HRV)
www.lunoscanada.com

Miele (Steam oven and in-wall coffee machine)
www.mieleusa.com

Method Homes (medicine cabinet)

Nest (thermostat and smoke detector)
www.nest.com

Sierra Pacific (doors and windows)
www.sierrapacificwindows.com

Taymor (bathroom accessories)
www.taymor.com/en

Toto (toilet)
www.totousa.com

WAC (lights)
www.waclighting.com

MSI Surfaces (kitchen solid surfacing)
www.msisurfaces.com

SOLEY HOUSE

Bertazzoni (double-wall oven and microwave)
www.us.bertazzoni.com

Broan (telescopic downdraft)
www.broan-nutone.com

Chilton (furniture)
www.chiltons.com

Daikin (heat recovery ventilator—HRV)
www.daikin.com

Dewey's Lumber and Cedar Mill (exterior cedar siding)
www.deweyslumber.com

Hancock Lumber (kitchen cabinetry)
www.hancocklumber.com

Huber Engineered Woods (sheathing)
www.huberwood.com

Performance Building Supply (doors)
www.performancebuildingsupply.com

Samsung (refrigerator)
www.samsung.com

Schueco (triple-pane windows)
www.schueco.com

Tesla (charging station)
www.tesla.com/supercharger

Thomas Moser (furniture)
www.thosmoser.com

PASSIVE HOUSE LA

Bosch (appliances)
www.bosch.us

Cavity sliders (pocket doors)
www.cavitysliders.com

Certainteed (dry wall)
www.certainteed.com

Four Seventy Five (PH products)
www.foursevenfive.com

Knauf Insulation (glass mineral wool insulation)
www.knaufinsulation.com

Kohler (bathroom supplies)
www.us.kohler.com/us

Metal Sales Manufacturing Corporation (metal siding)
www.metalsales.us.com

Mitsubishi (mini-split heating and cooling system)
www.mitsubishielectric.com

Rockwool (continuous insulation)
www.rockwool.com

Small Planet Supply (PH products)
www.smallplanetsupply.com

Stiebel Eltron (heat pump water heater)
www.stiebel-eltron-usa.com

Tesla (storage battery)
www.tesla.com/powerwall

Warema (exterior venetian blinds)
www.warema.com/en

Zhender America (HRV)
www.zhenderamerica.com

Zola (windows)
www.zolawindows.com

THE PINE HOUSE

Benjamin Moore (paint)
www.benjaminmoore.com

Caesarstone (quartz countertop)
www.caesarstoneus.com

Daltile (bathroom tile)
www.daltile.com

Fisher & Paykel (refrigerator)
www.fisherpaykel.com/us

Frigidaire (induction cooktop)
www.thermador.com

Grohe (faucets)
www.grohe.us

Marvin (windows and doors)
www.marvin.com

Mirabelle (bathtub)
www.ferguson.com

Ragnar Handcrafted Furniture (butcher-block countertop)
www.ragnarfurniture.com

Whirlpool (convection oven)
www.whirlpool.com

GLAD HOUSE

Daikin (mini-split heat pump)
www.daikincomfort.com

Fireclay Tile (backsplash)
www.fireclaytile.com

HardiePanel (siding)
www.jameshardie.com

IBC (tankless water heater)
www.ibcboiler.com

Midland Appliances (appliances)
www.midlandappliance.com

Venmar (HRV)
www.venmar.ca

Vetta Windows (windows)
www.vettawindows.com

DOG HOUSE

Benjamin Moore (paint)
www.benjaminmoore.com

Kohltech Windows and Entrance
Systems (windows and doors)
www.kohltech.com

LG (air-source heat pumps)
www.lghvac.com

Stala (interior doors)
www.stalabuildingsolutions.ca

Truefoam (insulation)
www.truefoam.com

Venmar (HRV)
www.venmar.ca

Vic West (metal roof tiles)
www.vicwest.com

HYGGE HOUSE

American Standard (plumbing
fixtures)
www.americanstandard-us.com

Ashley Norton (interior door
hardware)
www.ashleynorton.com

Bosch (appliances)
www.bosch-home.com/us

Duravit (plumbing fixtures)
www.duravit.us

Hansgrohe (plumbing fixtures)
www.hansgrohe-usa.com

Marvin Windows & Doors (windows
and doors)
www.marvin.com

Moen (plumbing fixtures)
www.moen.com

Ortal (heating gas fireplace)
www.ortalheat.com

Rinnai (heat pump)
www.rinnai.us

Schoolhouse Electric (LED lighting)
www.schoolhouse.com

Silestone (countertops)
www.silestoneusa.com

MICRO HOME

Daltile (tile)
www.daltile.com

Duravit (tub and toilet)
www.duravit.us

Emtek (door hardware)
www.emtek.com

GE (range)
www.geappliances.com

Grohe (kitchen faucet)
www.grohe.us

Hansgrohe (bathroom hardware)
www.hansgrohe-usa.com

Marvin (windows)
www.marvin.com

Summit (under-counter refrigerator)
www.summitappliance.com

Vigo (undermount kitchen sink)
www.vigoindustries.com

GEORGIA CEDAR HOUSE

BluDot (furnishings)
www.bludot.com

Design Within Reach (furnishings)
www.dwr.com

GE Monogram (stove)
www.geappliances.com

KitchenAid (refrigerator and
dishwasher)
www.kitchenaid.com

Room and Board (furnishings)
www.www.roomandboard.com

Serena & Lily (furnishings)
www.serenaandlily.com

Trade Wind (exhaust fan)
www.t-wusa.com

Wood Hollow Cabinets (kitchen
cabinets)
www.woodhollowcabinets.com

ALLEY CAT

Andersen Windows (windows)
www.andersenwindows.com

Eames (wire chairs)
www.hermanmiller.com

Elkay (stainless steel sink)
www.elkay.com/us/en.html

Fakro (pivot roof windows)
www.fakrousa.com

Haiku (ceiling fan)
www.bigassfans.com

Hansgrohe (bathroom showerhead
and faucets)
www.hansgrohe-usa.com

IKEA (appliances)
www.ikea.com

Kohler (soaking tub)
www.us.kohler.com/us/

La Cantina (multi-slide door)
www.lacantinadoors.com

Modern Forms (circle LED outdoor
wall light)
www.modernforms.com

Nelson (saucer pendant)
www.lumens.com

Nu-Ray (metal siding)
www.nuraymetals.com

Talis (kitchen faucet)
www.hansgrohe-usa.com

Toto (dual flush toilet)
www.totousa.com

BOHICKET HOUSE

Aquatica (lap pool)
www.aquaticapoolsandspas.com

Cummins (generator)
www.cummins.com

Fleetwood Windows & Doors
(impact glass)
www.fleetwoodusa.net

Rinnai (tankless water heaters)
www.rinnai.us

Scotsman (ice maker)
www.scotsman-ice.it

Shannon Horning Woodworks (all
built-in cabinets/paneling)
www.horningwoodworks.com

Thermador (refrigerator and
dishwasher)
www.thermador.com

Wolf (cooktop)
www.subzero-wolf.com

SEA RANCH HOUSE

Ann Sacks (backsplash tile)
www.annsacks.com

Fleetwood (glass doors)
www1.fleetwoodusa.com

Hansgrohe (faucet)
www.hansgrohe-usa.com

Herman Miller (lighting)
www.hermanmiller.com

Jøtul (direct-vent gas stove)
www.jotul.com

Ligne Roset (lighting and furniture)
www.ligne-roset.com/us/

Milgard (windows)
www.milgard.com

Porcelanosa (bathroom tile)
www.porcelanosa-usa.com

Stonco (lighting fixtures)

Sugatsune (cabinetry hardware)
www.sugatsune.com

WAC Lighting (lighting fixtures)
www.waclighting.com

Wolf (stove and hood)
www.subzero-wolf.com

TRIPLE BARN HOUSE

ABC Carpet & Home (nightstand)
www.abchome.com

Accent Windows and Doors
(windows)
www.accentwindowsct.com

B&B Italia (sofa)
www.bebitalia.com

The Butler & The Chef (outdoor
antique dining chairs)
www.butler-and-chef.com/

Design Within Reach (bed)
www.dwr.com

DURAME (coffee table)
www.durame.it/en/

Duravit (sinks and toilets)
www.duravit.us

Fermob (lounge chair, outdoor
dining table)
www.fermob.com/en

Garza Marfa (dining chairs)
www.garzamarfa.com

Hansgrohe (bathroom faucets)
www.hansgrohe-usa.com

IKEA (guest sink bathroom fixtures)
www.ikea.com

Lacava (main bath sink)
www.lacava.com

Modernica (dressers)
www.modernica.net

Nanimarquina (rug)
www.nanimarquina.com

Pablo (lamps)
www.pablodesigns.eu

STUA (chair)
www.stua.com/

Wittus (woodstove)
www.wittus.com

LITTLE BLACK HOUSE

Alpen (high-performance windows)
www.thinkalpen.com

Blomberg (compact washer and heat
pump ventless dryer)
www.blombergappliances.com

Bosch (dishwasher and range)
www.bosch-home.com/us

Duravit (bathroom sinks)
www.duravit.us

Emtek (door hardware)
www.emtek.com

Fisher and Paykel (refrigerator)
www.fisherpaykel.com/us

Grohe (kitchen and bathroom faucets)
www.grohe.us

Kohler (kitchen sink, toilets, and cast-
iron bathtub)
www.us.kohler.com/us

Marvin Integrity (doors)
www.marvin.com

Mitsubishi (air-source heat pump)
www.mitsubishicomfort.com

Morsø (woodstove)
www.morsoe.com/us/

Nora (mudroom and half-bath
commercial rubber flooring)
www.nora.com

State (electric hybrid heat pump
water heater)
www.statewaterheaters.com

Zehnder (heat recovery
ventilator—HRV)
www.zehnderamerica.com

Zephyr (range hood)
www.zephyronline.com

BUTTERFLY GARDEN COTTAGE

Azalea Lane (Windsor Park hickory
flooring)
www.azalealaneflooring.com

Circa Lighting (light fixtures)
www.circalighting.com

Daltile (tile)
www.daltile.com

Delta (water fixtures)
www.deltafaucet.com

Electrolux (washer/dryer)
www.electroluxappliances.com

Frigidaire (dishwasher)
www.frigidaire.com

Nichiha (fiber cement siding)
www.nichiha.com

Overhead Door (garage door)
www.overheaddoor.com

Plygem Windows (all windows)
www.plygem.com/windows-doors/

Rinnai (tankless water heater)
www.rinnai.us

Sentrigard (metal roofing)
www.sentrigard.com

Sherwin Williams (paint)
www.sherwin-williams.com

Timberlake (kitchen cabinets)
www.timberlake.com

Thermador (refrigerator)
www.thermador.com/us

Wolf (stove)
www.subzero-wolf.com

ROME DRIVE HOUSE

Abet Laminati (shelves: Douglas fir
plywood, plastic laminate)
www.abetlaminati.com/en/

Caesarstone (kitchen island)
www.caesarstoneus.com

Elfa (pantry shelves)
www.elfa.com/en

Elkay (sink)
www.elkay.com/us/en.html

Frigidaire (refrigerator)
www.frigidaire.com

Franke (hood)
www.franke.com

Grohe (faucet)
www.grohe.us

IKEA (cabinets with vertical grain
Douglas fir plywood doors)
www.ikea.com

Miele (dishwasher, oven, cooktop)
www.mieleusa.com

M'S HOUSE

Distinctive Wood (kitchen cabinets
and closets)
www.distinctivecabinet.com

IKEA (bath vanity cabinets)
www.ikea.com

James Hardie (fiber cement siding)
www.jameshardie.com

Kolbe (windows and doors)
www.kolbewindows.com

Lifebreath (HRV)
www.lifebreath.com

LivingStone (countertops)
www.livingstonesurfaces.com

Modern Forms (bath sconces)
www.modernforms.com

Navien (tankless gas water heater)
www.navieninc.com

Nelson (pendant light in dining room)
www.hay.dk/en

Regency Horizon (gas fireplace)
www.regency-fire.com

Thermador (gas range)
www.thermador.com

Zephyr (kitchen hood)
www.zephyronline.com

THE SCOTT HOUSE

CDM Windows (triple-pane windows)
www.cdmwindowsanddoor.com

Ecocor (insulated Passive foundation
and Passive wall panels)
www.ecocor.us

IKEA (kitchen cabinets)
www.ikea.com/us/en

Lamco (wood planks for upstairs and
exposed ceiling)
www.lemcodesign.com

Mitsubishi (air-source heat pump for
heating and cooling)
www.mitsubishicomfort.com

Sun Bandit (hot water heater)
www.www.sunbandit.us

Zehnder (energy recovery
ventilator—ERV)
www.zehnderamerica.com

BOW HILL HOUSE

Andersen (glass bi-fold doors)
www.andersenwindows.com

Broan (energy recovery system—ERV)
www.broan-nutone.com

Crate & Barrel (furnishings and rug)
www.crateandbarrel.com

Daikin (heat pump)
www.northamerica-daikin.com

GE (appliances)
www.geappliances.com

Graypants (dining room lights)
www.graypants.com

Heat & Glo (direct vent gas fireplace)
www.heatnglo.com

Hinkley Lighting (island lights)
www.hinkleylightinglights.com

Silestone (quartz countertop)
www.silestoneusa.com

SmartSun (window glazing)
www.andersenwindows.com

Thermador (kitchen hood)
www.thermador.com

West Elm (framed mirror)
www.westelm.com

LITTLE RED HOUSE

Ashley Norton (hardware)
www.ashleynorton.com

Benjamin Moore (paint)
www.benjaminmoore.com

Bosch (dishwasher)
www.bosch-home.com

Daltile (tile)
www.daltile.com

Duravit (bathroom sink)
www.duravit.us

Elkay (kitchen sink)
www.elkay.com

Heath (tile)
www.heathceramics.com

IKEA (kitchen cabinets)
www.ikea.com/us/en

I Love Wallpaper (bedroom wallpaper)
www.ilovewallpaper.com/wallpaper

Kohler (faucets)
www.us.kohler.com/us

Limitless Walls (Bathroom mural in
the public domain image from the
Library of Congress of a 1904 Ernst
Haeckel print)
www.limitlesswalls.com

Miele (induction range)
www.mieleusa.com

Niagara (toilets)
www.niagaracorp.com

Wow (tile)
www.wowdesigneu.com

Zephyr (kitchen hood)
www.zephyronline.com

BLANCO RIVER HOUSE

Bosch (dishwasher)
www.bosch-home.com

Grohe (plumbing fixtures)
www.grohe.us

Samsung (electric oven and range,
hood, refrigerator)
www.samsung.com/us/
home-appliances/

Sherwin Williams (paint)
www.sherwin-williams.com

Silestone (quartz countertops)
www.silestoneusa.com

TREE HOUSE

Bertazzoni (range)
www.us.bertazzoni.com

Bosch (dishwasher)
www.bosch-home.com/us

Caesarstone (countertops)
www.caesarstoneus.com

Carrier (ductless mini-split units)
www.carrier.com

Fleetwood (windows)
www.fleetwoodusa.com

James Hardie (fiber cement siding)
www.jameshardie.com

Miele (induction cooktop)
www.mieleusa.com